Secrets
of the
Congdon Mansion

Jaykay Publishing
White Bear Lake, MN

Jaykay Publishing
White Bear, MN
ISBN 978-0-961-37782-3
Printed in U.S.A.
Revised 2004

The Introduction

Don't expect to get all your questions answered when you take a tour of Glensheen, the Congdon Mansion in Duluth. For the real story about the murders and the family intrigue and the decades-long aftermath, you need more information than the tour guides can reveal. You need the information available here in *Secrets of the Congdon Mansion*.

You'll also find an entire section – Inside Stories – with never-before published tales that I've told over the years to friends and family about the fascinating characters in the case, along with the story's many twists and turns.

The Official Tour through the mansion, of course, is very worthwhile. You'll learn that the 39-room home is a striking example of Jacobean architecture. You'll be told about the design and décor of the building and you'll see state of the art woodwork and furnishings from the early 1900s.

But for many of us, those aren't the main reasons for visiting Glensheen; we're paying for mystery.

The mansion was the site of the infamous Congdon Murders. It's where 83-year-old heiress Elisabeth Congdon was murdered June 27, 1977, smothered in her bed with a pink satin pillow.

Miss Congdon's night nurse also was killed that night, beaten to death with a candlestick holder as she tried to protect the defenseless dowager.

The prosecutor called it a crime of greed. The murderer wanted to speed up his share of the vast estate, he said.

It was a complex and intriguing murder case. At times, the plot seemed to leap from the pages of an Agatha Christie novel and each succeeding chapter made front-page news throughout Minnesota. It catered, somehow, to the public's fascination with murder and mansions and money.

But you won't get the entire story on the Official Tour. The guides much prefer to talk about the family's philanthropy and the garden and the architecture. For decades they were instructed not to reveal which bedroom was Miss Congdon's or where the murderer broke into the house or how he escaped.

That's the reason for this book, to answer those questions and more; to tell you the *Secrets of the Congdon Mansion*.

The Intruder

*I*n a cemetery next to the mansion he waited, huddled next to a tree, trying to stay out of sight. He was jumpy, drunk and desperate. The instructions ran through his mind. Through the woods, he heard cars race by on London Road, busy even then, in the wee hours of morning. Behind him, waves from Lake Superior broke along the shore, steady, insistent, growing louder, he thought, with each passing minute.

Finally, after more than an hour, he steeled his nerve and clenched his teeth. It was time. He took one last swig from the bottle in his pocket, then walked slowly to the lake side of the mansion. He soon found the covered patio area – the place the family called the subway. The windows had been removed for the summer, so he stepped right in.

Using a rock, he broke a hole in the window of the billiard room. He reached inside, unlatched the window and opened it wide. He climbed into the room, then paused a moment and listened. Nothing stirred.

Stepping gingerly, sometimes crunching the broken glass strewn on the floor, he felt his way around the large billiard table and walked out into the hallway. Still no alarm.

Around to the right he found the stairs, just as he'd been told. Quietly, gently he went up, step by step. He made it to the main floor. Just one more flight and he'd find the bedroom of Elisabeth Congdon, his wealthy mother-in-law.

The plan was simple. Miss Congdon was 83, her right side was paralyzed. No one would be surprised if she died one night in her sleep. All he had to do was make sure tonight was the night, then he'd slip unnoticed out the door and return to Colorado. When all the probate details were worked out – in a suitable, but hopefully short, period after the funeral – he and his wife would receive their inheritance worth millions, more than enough to pay off the thousands of dollars in debt that were piling up back home.

(Later, he denied that he planned to murder the old lady. He said he wanted to burglarize the mansion and sell the stolen items to pay off the bills. And some speculate that he wasn't alone, that a cohort from Colorado came with him to help with the job. But police investigators maintain that he was alone and that murder was the mission.)

Climbing slowly, he neared the top of the stairway. He stumbled, breaking his trance. He pulled out the pint of vodka and took another drink to restore his resolve. He shook his head to clear the tangled knot of liquor and fear and started back up the stairs.

Suddenly, a door opened in the hallway above.

A ribbon of light swept past him. A woman with a flashlight came to the door, probing the darkness. She screamed. He shouted. They struggled for a moment on the stairs but she was old and much smaller; he overpowered her easily. He flung her down toward the landing, midway between floors. This wasn't part of the plan, he thought, shivering with fear. He raced to the top of the stairs, more anxious than ever to finish the job and be gone.

But from below, on the landing, the woman moaned. He had to stop that noise. From a table at the head of the stairs he found a 12-inch brass candlestick holder and walked slowly toward the moaning woman. He beat her on the head and arms, fracturing her skull and breaking her jaw on both sides. Reaching out in blind defense, she clawed at the attacker's head and pulled out several locks of his hair. She clutched the hair tightly in her hands as she died.

Bloodied from the unexpected encounter, the killer rushed up the stairs and found his target – Miss Congdon's bedroom – the first door around to the right. The old woman should have been asleep, but was awakened by the racket from below.

"Who's there?" she asked.

The killer didn't reply, but pulled a pillow from beneath her head and held it firmly against her face. Terrified, she tried to resist. She fought vigorously with her attacker, turning her head from side to side. Skin from her nose rubbed off on the pillowcase as she struggled for her life. It took nearly four minutes, but then she, too, was dead.

The killer methodically opened all the drawers in the bedroom. He found a small, wicker basket in the back of the closet and filled it with jewelry from the bureau and dresser. From the dead woman's finger he took a sapphire and diamond ring, from her wrist he took a gold watch. Those, too, went into the basket. As he started to leave, he noticed a gold coin in a memorabilia box. He took that, too.

He ducked into a small bathroom across the hall and washed his bloody hands, wiping them on his shirt and pants, which were already streaked with blood. On a bed in an adjoining bedroom he saw a purse. Inside was a set of keys – the nurse's car, he thought. Grabbing them, he ran down the steps, past the dead woman lying across the window seat on the landing.

He left through the front door and matched the keys to the 1976 white and tan Ford Granada parked in the driveway. Then he drove to the Minneapolis-St. Paul airport, 175 miles away, stopping once to ask for directions.

∼

The Congdons

It was a hot Sunday afternoon at the Congdon Mansion on the shores of Lake Superior in Duluth. Elisabeth Congdon and her attendant had just returned from a weekend at the summer place, the family home on the Brule River in northwestern Wisconsin.

As Miss Congdon rested in her bedroom, one of the nurses unpacked the clothes from the trip and put a small wicker basket away in the closet. Miss Congdon went to sleep shortly before 11 p.m., without her usual medication. "She was tired and very happy and went right to sleep," the nurse said. It was June 26, 1977.

Those weekend trips away from the mansion weren't easy for Miss Congdon – or Miss Elisabeth as the staff affectionately called her. She was 83-years-old and still hobbled by a stroke that had caused partial paralysis eight years earlier. But she tried to keep a normal routine. She had some assistance: around-the-clock nurses and the best medical care money could buy. She was, after all, one of the richest women in Minnesota, the last remaining child of Chester Congdon, and heiress to his fortune.

Chester Congdon had been a legend in his time, known throughout northeastern Minnesota for building a fortune in the burgeoning iron mining business at the turn of the 20th century. Born in New York, he became a lawyer in 1877, then worked as a teacher in New York and was a school principal in Wisconsin for a short time. Next stop was St. Paul, where he joined a local law firm. He got a break a year later when he met the U.S. District Attorney and was hired as an assistant D.A. He married his college sweetheart, Clara, and began raising a family. Then he ran his own law firm in St. Paul for a while before moving to Duluth to join a larger firm. There he invested in large tracts of what appeared to be marginal iron producing land. When large steel companies later bought that land, Congdon's fortune was cinched. He later served in the Minnesota Legislature, and also invested in Arizona mining lands.

In 1905 he began building the mansion. The family called it Glensheen and it was the best money could buy. It cost $864,000 in 1908 dollars and was complete with marble and oak, gold leaf and teak trim, and furnishings from around the world. The property included 7½ beautifully landscaped acres, with a creek running through the property to the lake.

Elisabeth Congdon

Chester and Clara had seven children. Elisabeth, the youngest, was 14 when the family moved into the mansion in 1908. She went east, briefly, to Vassar College, but then returned to Duluth. Chester died in 1916 at the age of 61. Elisabeth was the only unmarried child, so she lived in the mansion with her mother. She was active in many charitable activities. She was the first president of Duluth's King's Daughters Society, which later became the Junior League of Duluth.

Even though she never married, Elisabeth adopted two daughters in the 1930s, an unusual event at the time. The two girls grew up at the mansion, with all the comforts of the rich. One daughter was Jennifer, who eventually married Charles Johnson, a successful businessman who founded a large electronics company. They lived a relatively normal life in Racine, Wisconsin.

The other daughter was Marjorie, whose life was far from normal.

Congdon notes:

Five years before her death, Elisabeth Congdon allowed the Mansion to be used as the location for the filming of the movie "You'll Like My Mother," starring Patty Duke and Richard Thomas. The film is about a young widow who visits her new mother-in-law in the family's large, spooky mansion. She doesn't realize, however, that her real mother-in-law has been murdered and that one of the killers is impersonating the dead woman.

Shortly after the real murders in the Mansion, a downtown Duluth theater revived the film for a short time. And because of the Congdon case, the video version generates a small, but steady business on Amazon.com/.

The Daughter

Marjorie lived in Colorado during the summer of 1977, in Golden, a suburb of Denver and the home of Coor's Beer. Her new husband, Roger Caldwell, was born and raised in Latrobe, Pennsylvania, the home of Rolling Rock Beer.

This was her second marriage. She met her first husband, Richard LeRoy, in St. Louis in 1950. They married a year later and had seven children. The marriage ended in 1971.

Marjorie had moved to Colorado in 1975 with her youngest son, Ricky. Her other children remained in Minnesota. She met Roger Caldwell, who was also divorced, at a Parents Without Partners meeting. They hit it off and were married two months later in March 1976.

Roger told his family that he didn't know about Marjorie's wealthy family for some time. Years later he told me about their first financial chat:

She told him: "I have some money."

He said: "Good, because I don't."

"No, really, Roger. I do."

"What do you mean by 'some money?'" he asked. When she told him about her family's fortunes, he said he almost fell over.

Marjorie did, indeed, have some money – at least in theory. Upon the death of her mother, Marjorie stood to inherit a good share of the Congdon estate. In addition, Miss Congdon had set up two trusts for Marjorie and her family in 1968. At one time, these trusts were worth more than $1 million. But Marjorie withdrew large sums from the trusts, as much as $105,000 in one year. Apparently she didn't always pay attention to the limits of her bank account.

In 1975, the bank handling the trusts asked a judge for permission to stop paying her bills, if the bank felt that the payments were not in the best interests of Marjorie or her family.

Marjorie had been known as a spendthrift throughout her life. When her daughters were young and interested in horses, she bought 300 to 350 riding outfits for them, when they really needed only three apiece, according to one of the daughters.

Marjorie Caldwell

In 1976, a Minneapolis judge wrote: "It is all too apparent from the evidence that Mrs. LeRoy (Marjorie) … tended to spend sums of money greatly in excess of the income available to her from the two trusts."

Congdon notes:

Marjorie's first husband, Richard LeRoy, was once chairman of the Minnesota T (Taxpayer's) Party and he was the Minneapolis chairman of Minnesotans for Goldwater in 1964. He was on the Minneapolis Library Board and ran unsuccessfully for the Minneapolis School Board in 1967.

The Son-In-Law

Roger Caldwell was raised in Latrobe, Pa., a small town near Pittsburgh. Roger's father worked in the steel mills all his life. Roger was one of four sons; one brother followed their father into the mill and became a supervisor, another was a college professor. The third was a local policeman.

Roger eloped with his childhood sweetheart in 1954, when he was 20. He spent some time in a seminary, then worked as a salesman in several different states. The couple had two daughters and eventually settled in Colorado. But he drank heavily and the marriage ended in divorce.

After his whirlwind marriage to Marjorie, the couple soon found themselves in financial trouble. Marjorie kept up her torrid spending pace. In late 1976 and early 1977, she signed contracts for more than $750,000 worth of Colorado ranch land. But all the deals eventually fell through when she failed to come up with the money. In several cases, she told real estate agents that her mother was wealthy and would pay for the transactions.

The Caldwells were apparently desperate when Roger flew to Duluth, alone, on May 25, 1977, for his first meeting with his mother-in-law, Elisabeth Congdon. During the visit, Roger spent half an hour at the Congdon Mansion, chatting with Miss Congdon. They talked in the library on the main floor of the house, just inside the front door. That was the only part of the house that Roger saw that day.

He did not discuss money with Miss Congdon, although that was the point of his visit. He knew she no longer handled her own financial matters. Financial trustees had taken over those duties a few years before, after Marjorie had convinced her mother to make several questionable payments.

So Roger met with the trustees to make his plea. He told them he needed $800,000 so that he and Marjorie could buy a ranch. He even produced a letter from a prominent physician, stating that Marjorie's youngest son, Ricky, needed to live in the mountains because of an asthma condition. The letter, it turned out later, was forged.

The trustees turned down Roger's request. A week later, Roger met with another Congdon family member in Denver, again asking for money. Roger told the man that

Roger Caldwell

he and Marjorie were desperately short of cash and had even used slugs in a pop machine. They needed $81,000 right away to pay off debts, or else they could land in jail.

But once again, Roger returned empty handed.

Congdon notes:

Latrobe is best known as the hometown of golfer Arnold Palmer and Fred (Mr.) Rogers from public television's children's series. Roger ran track and played football in high school.

The Scene
of the Crime

At 7 a.m., on the dot, the morning nurse reported for duty at the Congdon Mansion. It was Monday, June 27, 1977.

Nurse Mildred Garvue was scheduled to relieve her old friend, Velma Pietila, who'd spent the night at the mansion, caring for Miss Congdon. Velma had retired as a Congdon nurse in May, but had agreed to fill in on the Sunday overnight shift, because one of the regular nurses was on vacation and another had company.

When Nurse Garvue arrived, she stopped in the kitchen to get some medicine for Miss Congdon, then headed up the stairs towards the bedroom. She saw Velma's body lying across the window seat on the landing. She wondered if Velma was resting, then worried that she'd had a stroke. She checked for a pulse. There was none. Then, she realized that Miss Congdon was upstairs, alone. She ran up to the bedroom and saw a pillow over the heiress's face.

Fearing the worst, she looked under the pillow and realized that Miss Congdon was dead. She ran downstairs, told the maid, and then called police. Worried that the murderer might still be in the house, the two women waited anxiously in the main hallway for help to arrive.

Police arrived, searched the house and the grounds, then began interviewing the household staff. Loren Pietila, Velma's husband, was called and told to hurry to the mansion. He couldn't believe his wife was dead, and told Ernie Grams, Duluth's Chief of Detectives, that he had asked her not to work that night. Talking further, Grams realized that the car Velma drove to work that night was missing.

Publicly, police called it a robbery. "An empty jewelry box was on the floor of the bedroom and the room was ransacked," Grams told the media.

But behind the scenes, police already were tracking two prime suspects: Marjorie and Roger Caldwell. Immediately upon hearing the news, family members told police that they suspected the Caldwells, primarily because of the couple's financial troubles.

Within hours after the murders were discovered a Congdon relative in Denver hired a private investigator to protect his family from the Caldwells.

Based on the tips from the family, Duluth police began an intense investigation in Duluth and in Colorado. They checked out the Holland House Motel in Golden, Colo., where the Caldwells were living. When the Caldwells attended Miss Congdon's

Ernie Grams

funeral, they stayed at the Radisson Hotel in Duluth. Police checked out that room, too. And they checked the Holiday Inn Airport South in Bloomington, where the couple stayed for several nights after the funeral.

At each place, police found evidence that firmed up the case against the Caldwells. It was enough, they believed, to link Roger to the murder.

My colleagues and I covering the case for the Minneapolis Tribune discovered much of this evidence, too. And even though police still maintained publicly that it was a botched burglary case as late as July 5, we prepared a story for the July 6 editions naming Roger Caldwell – Miss Congdon's son-in-law – as the chief suspect.

Because of a deal I'd made with Detective Grams, I called to let him know we were running the story. He wasn't happy and said: "Now we'll have to lay all our cards on the table."

About midnight, Grams called me at home to say that Roger Caldwell had been arrested in a suburban Minneapolis hospital room. He had collapsed in a Bloomington hotel room the day before and was recovering when police arrived.

I called the newspaper and despite the late hour was able to change the story. The new headline on the morning editions read: Son-in-law arrested in Congdon murder case.

Congdon notes:

Early in the investigation I wrote a feature story about Ernie Grams as he worked long hours to solve the case. Trying to find a colorful phrase to describe him, I called him the "Duluth Sleuth." He was very helpful to a rookie reporter trying to cover this major case, and I'd spend hours a day outside his office, watching him chomp on his ever-present cigar. Other agencies that worked with him on the case were: the State Patrol, Golden, Colo. police, Twin Cities airport police, police officers from Twin Cities suburbs of Fridley, Bloomington and St. Louis Park, and the Hennepin County Sheriff's deputies.

The State vs.
Roger Caldwell

While Roger waited in jail, a judge ruled that too much publicity in the case meant Caldwell could not receive a fair trial in Duluth, so the trial was moved to Brainerd, a growing resort town in north central Minnesota.

Jury selection began in April 1978, ten months after the murders. Attorneys spent nearly a month questioning 81 potential jurors, before seven women and five men were selected.

Then Prosecutor John DeSanto moved into action, methodically presenting the case of the State of Minnesota vs. Roger Sipe Caldwell.

There was no direct evidence linking Caldwell to the crimes. There were no eyewitnesses or fingerprints on the candlestick holder. But DeSanto presented 100 witnesses whose testimony wove a web of circumstantial evidence, which, DeSanto alleged, proved that Caldwell was guilty beyond a reasonable doubt.

The motive was greed, he said. The Caldwells were so deep in debt that they needed the inheritance to pay their bills. And even in their penniless state, they continued to shop for a ranch in the mountains. A sudden infusion of cash was the only way they'd ever pay for that.

A stream of witnesses outlined the Caldwells' financial woes: repossessed Jeeps, the trip to Duluth to plead for money, the ranch deals that fell through for lack of a down payment.

"This was a very extravagant, spendthrift, dream-world type lifestyle for this unemployed fortune seeker," DeSanto told the jury. "And this financial pressure continued to build until that fatal day." Caldwell, sitting at the defense table near the front of the courtroom, remained impassive during this stinging rebuke.

DeSanto told the jury about a piece of paper found in the Caldwells' safe deposit, which appeared to be a will, made out by Marjorie just three days before the murder. The will gave Roger control of more than $2.5 million of his wife's expected inheritance. DeSanto called the will "the carrot," intended to entice Roger to commit the murders.

Some key evidence presented in the trial:

- A wicker basket, filled with jewelry, which police found in the Caldwells' Bloomington motel room after Miss Congdon's funeral. It was the same jewelry

John DeSanto

and basket taken from the closet in Miss Congdon's bedroom, a Congdon employee told the jury.

- A gold coin, the Byzantine coin that was taken from Miss Congdon's bedroom on the night of the murders. Bizarrely, police found the coin in an unopened envelope inside the Caldwells' mailbox at their motel in Golden. It had been postmarked in Duluth on June 27, the day of the murders, and delivered in Colorado while the Caldwells were in Duluth for the funeral. Experts said the envelope was addressed to Roger Caldwell in his own handwriting. And Roger's thumbprint was on the envelope, too, according to the testimony of a fingerprint expert. DeSanto told the jury that this was proof Roger had been in Duluth that day, and that he'd probably mailed the coin to Colorado as a signal to Marjorie that the deed had been done.

- A receipt for $56 from the Minneapolis-St. Paul Airport gift shop, found in the Caldwells' Duluth hotel room after the funeral. Police said the receipt, dated June 27, was for a suede suit bag, which police later found in the Caldwells' Bloomington hotel room. The receipt was crucial to the case because it showed Roger had been in Minnesota on the day of the murders.

- The prosecution had some unexpected help in the case when two employees of the airport gift shop, testifying under oath about the receipt, pointed to Roger in the courtroom and said he was the man who'd purchased the suede bag on the morning after the murders. Spectators in the courtroom were aghast, because earlier in the trial DeSanto had told the jurors that neither of the two employees could specifically remember Roger or identify him. But sitting at the witness stand, each one calmly pointed to Roger and said he was the man she'd seen in the gift shop nearly a year earlier. It was like a scene from a television courtroom drama when defense attorney Doug Thomson tried to discredit the witnesses by pointing out to the jury that the clerks had failed to identify Roger when questioned by police four days after the murder, when their memories, presumably, were much clearer.

But there were several holes in the state's case. The major one was proving how Caldwell got back to Colorado. Several witnesses in Golden, including a banker, testified that they'd seen Roger Caldwell in Colorado late in the day of the murders. For that to be true (if Roger committed the murders), it appears there were only two commercial air flights from Minneapolis that he could have taken early that morning. Police checked airline records for both flights but could not find Roger's name or a likely alias.

Prosecutors worked hard to overcome this obstacle and finally decided that the banker was wrong; that Roger had come to the bank to try to get his repossessed Jeep back on the following day. But the banker, with full confidence that he was right, was a difficult witness to refute.

And Ricky LeRoy, Marjorie's youngest son from her first marriage, was living with the Caldwells in Golden and testified that he looked into the bedroom the night of the murders and saw "two lumps under the covers." But he said he had not seen Roger's face and his testimony, coming from a 17-year-old who was clearly supporting his mother throughout the case, was not particularly harmful to the prosecution.

Still, many serious questions remained about the case against Roger. If he had killed the women, why did he bring the stolen jewelry back to Colorado, then pack it up again and bring it to the Twin Cities?

And why did he mail the gold coin to himself? None of his fingerprints were found inside the mansion, so why was he so careful there, but then was so careless to leave prints on the coin's envelope?

Why did he rely on nurse Pietila's car for the get-away? Pietila was filling in that night for a vacationing nurse. How did he know her car, or any car, would be available?

Defense attorney Thomson pointed to these inconsistencies in the case, all of which suggested that Caldwell had been framed. He knew that the rest of the Congdons did not like Marjorie, and suggested to the jury that they might have arranged to make it look like Marjorie's new husband was the killer. (He conveniently neglected to say how any of Miss Congdon's other relatives could be so heartless as to murder their beloved matriarch just to frame the family's bad seed.)

DeSanto told the jury that Roger made "stupid moves" because he "wasn't himself after the murders, or maybe he was feeling a false sense of security because he thought he had gotten away with it."

One other apparent hole in the prosecution's case was cleared up before the trial ended. Police had found two fingerprints at the mansion that apparently didn't match up with anyone involved in the case. They definitely weren't Roger's, and Thomson hinted that they might belong to the real killer.

Police checked further, though, and cleared up the mystery. One of the fingerprints belonged to a part-time nurse at the mansion.

The other print – found on the blood-stained bathroom sink where the killer had washed before fleeing the mansion– belonged to Duluth Police Sgt. Gary Waller, the chief investigator in the case.

Doug Thomson

Testimony in the trial lasted two months. Finally, on July 6, 1978, the jurors began deliberations. They spent three days in a small room in Brainerd's Crow Wing County courthouse, arguing back and forth.

It wasn't until 4:30 p.m. on the third day that they reached a consensus. The courtroom was silent as the jurors marched in, taking their places in the jury box. The court clerk took the verdict and read the word: "Guilty."

Roger Caldwell, who had not testified in his own defense, looked at the jurors and softly said: "You're wrong."

The judge asked each of the jurors if they agreed with the verdict. All 12 said yes. One woman cried as she replied.

Later, several jurors said the sentiment in the jury room initially seemed to be for acquittal. But by the time the first vote was taken, it was seven to five for guilty. The discussions continued until everyone agreed with the judgment of guilt.

Two days later, Roger Caldwell was sentenced to two consecutive life terms in prison. St. Louis County Judge Jack Litman called the murders "brutal, heinous, awful and awesome."

The day after Roger's sentencing, the other shoe dropped. Marjorie Caldwell was charged with conspiring with her husband to kill her mother and the nurse. She turned herself in to Duluth police and was quickly released on $100,000 bond.

Part Two of the Congdon Murder Trials had begun.

The State vs. Marjorie Caldwell

A s Marjorie prepared for trial, another judge ruled that there had been too much publicity in the case for her to get a fair trial in Duluth. So Marjorie's trial was moved to Hastings, a small town on the edge of St. Paul's southern suburbs.

In the beginning, the Marjorie trial was similar to Roger's trial. Jury selection was lengthy, taking nearly three weeks. And again, John DeSanto was the prosecutor.

Testimony began on April 26, 1979. DeSanto again told of the Caldwells' extravagant lifestyle and subsequent debts. And we learned a little more about their personal relationship. DeSanto told jurors that Marjorie "dominated and manipulated Roger from the very beginning." She planned the murders, he committed them "with the assurance he would get a certain amount of the money," DeSanto said.

Much of DeSanto's evidence in this trial was familiar: financial documents, the suit bag, the gold coin and stolen jewelry. In addition, he outlined conflicting stories Marjorie had told about Roger's whereabouts on the night of the murders. She told her son Ricky that she and Roger would be looking at real estate all weekend. She told a real estate agent that Roger was in Colorado Springs, she told a lawyer that Roger had just gone to a convenience store and she told someone else that Roger was visiting a sick friend at a Denver hospital, DeSanto said.

The defense in this trial was much more aggressive. Ron Meshbesher, Marjorie's attorney, had used the year since Roger's trial well; he had some surprises for the prosecution. Meshbesher began by attacking the police investigation of the case. Under cross-examination by Meshbesher, a police officer admitted that he'd used the toilet and sink in the upstairs bathroom while searching for evidence. Other police officers said that they lost photographs taken during the investigation, and when duplicates were made there was confusion about who took the photos and when they were taken. Meshebesher seem to take pride in making the police look like bumbling idiots.

Marjorie's former lawyer, David Arnold, caused quite a stir when he testified that Marjorie "loved her mother and never spoke an unkind word about her." Arnold also said that Marjorie thought she might not inherit much of the Congdon estate because she was adopted.

An even bigger stir arose during testimony about William Furman, a Colorado private investigator. Within hours of the murders, Congdon family members living

Ronald Meshbesher

in Denver hired Furman to protect them, fearing that Roger and Marjorie might be on a rampage. Later Furman said he was told to investigate the Caldwells. During that investigation, Furman and his associates supposedly followed the Caldwells from Golden to Duluth and then to Bloomington. In each of those places, evidence that incriminated the Caldwells was found and used against them. Meshbesher hinted to the jury that Furman might have planted that evidence as part of an elaborate scheme to frame the Caldwells for the murders.

Duluth police were also aware of Furman's investigation, but soon discounted its value. They suspected that Furman never even went to Duluth or Bloomington, but merely submitted a bill for the expenses in an attempt to defraud Thomas Congdon.

Furman indirectly confirmed those suspicions when he was called to the witness stand. He refused to answer 59 questions put to him, claiming his Fifth Amendment right against self-incrimination. Furman remained a mystery man in the case.

Another surprise came late in the trial when a Golden, Colorado waitress testified that she had seen Roger Caldwell in Golden only hours before the murders were committed. Waitress Candace Byers said she saw Roger coming down the stairs of the Holland House Motel at 10 p.m. Mountain Time on the evening before the murders. If that was true, it appeared highly unlikely that Roger – who didn't seem to have access to a private jet – could have made it to Duluth in time to kill the women later that night.

Byers' testimony came as a shock to the prosecution. She had not testified in Roger's trial. And when questioned by police just days after the murders, nearly two years earlier, Byers said she had last seen Roger two days before the women were killed. She said nothing about seeing him the night of the murders. At the trial, she explained her confusion to the jury: "I was real nervous talking to the police. I just wanted them to leave. I had customers waiting for me and they were staring at me."

She had changed, or embellished, her story just three months before Marjorie's trial, when questioned by Meshbesher's investigators as they prepared for the second trial. Even then, she didn't tell police about her new memory. She said the investigators "asked her not to pass it around."

Perhaps the biggest blow to the prosecution's case, though, came when a fingerprint expert from Maryland, hired by DeSanto, testified that the thumbprint on the envelope containing the gold coin was not Roger Caldwell's print.

That thumbprint had been a huge factor in Roger Caldwell's conviction. Experts swore it was his print and because of the Duluth postmark on the day of the murders, it pretty well cinched the prosecution's claim that Roger had been in Duluth that day. Some jurors in the first trial said the thumbprint helped them convict Roger. But this new testimony, which was even more devastating because it came from a prosecution witness, meant the thumbprint didn't count anymore and the case against Marjorie was looking a bit shaky.

During his final argument, Meshbesher wove an elaborate frame-up theory to convince the jury of Marjorie's innocence. Furman and his friends had planted the evidence, he said, so Marjorie would be deprived of her rightful inheritance. And to cover himself if the jury wasn't buying the frame, Meshbesher eloquently argued that even if Roger had killed the women, his wife knew nothing about it. Caldwell was a drunk, he said, and sometimes went on binges for days at a time.

The jury deliberated for nine hours. Marjorie sobbed quietly as jurors entered the courtroom. When the verdict "Not guilty" was read, she cried openly. Even Meshbesher had tears in his eyes. So did John DeSanto's mother, who'd been in the courtroom. But DeSanto eyes were angry, not misty.

After the trial, the jurors expressed sympathy for Marjorie and invited her to a party later in the week. She accepted, but didn't attend. Marjorie told reporters that she was tired and a little wobbly in the knees.

But her troubles were far from over.

The Inheritance

When Marjorie walked out of the Hastings courtroom she was a free woman, but not a rich one. Her share of the Congdon inheritance, estimated at up to $8 million, was still tied up in the courts.

Four of Marjorie's children had filed suit in 1977, trying to prevent her from sharing in Miss Congdon's wealth. They were relying on a state law that forbids anyone involved with a murder from inheriting money from the deceased.

This probate court matter dragged on even after Marjorie's acquittal in the criminal case. The State Supreme Court ruled that a civil trial to decide the inheritance issue could be held without subjecting Marjorie to double jeopardy.

Finally, before it could go to trial, Marjorie and her children settled out of court. On June 29, 1983, they agreed to share the money, which was significantly reduced when lawyers skimmed about $2 million off the top.

Under the agreement, Marjorie was to receive about $1.5 million from a trust left by her grandfather. The remainder, several millions more, would go to her children. Marjorie, though, will receive the interest from one-third of the children's share, as long as she lives. The children also shared a second trust, worth about $2 million. Attorney's fees and debts were deducted from the trusts.

In the mid-1980s, family members believed Marjorie was getting about $40,000 per year from the trusts.

When told of the financial arrangement in 1987, Roger Caldwell – then living on welfare in Pennsylvania – said: "No matter how much money she has, it will never be enough."

～

The Deal

After Marjorie's acquittal in Hastings, Roger Caldwell immediately appealed his conviction, claiming that new evidence from her trial – primarily the false thumbprint – would prove his innocence. The Minnesota Supreme Court agreed. On Aug. 7, 1982, the justices ordered a new trial. Roger had already been in custody for five years.

In their decision, the justices cited the thumbprint, which, you'll remember, was found on an envelope in the Caldwells' Colorado hotel. The envelope, which had been postmarked in Duluth on the day of the murder, contained a gold coin taken from Miss Congdon's bedroom. The thumbprint was a major factor in Roger's conviction, because it showed Roger had been in Duluth that day. At Marjorie's trial, though, the experts changed course and testified that it wasn't Roger's thumbprint, after all.

Prosecutor John DeSanto was shocked at the Supreme Court's ruling. "There's no question that we have the right man in jail," he said.

Roger was released from prison pending the new trial and returned home to Latrobe, Pa. On the day of his release he was asked about his plans. "Maybe I'll become a tour guide at the Congdon Mansion," he said. One of his relatives later noted that "Roger has a dark sense of humor."

At first, officials in Duluth vowed that they'd go after Roger again in court, convinced that they could get another conviction. But as the trial date approached, that resolve began to fade. In the end, neither side really wanted another trial. Roger didn't want to risk another conviction and the prosecutors hoped to avoid the cost of another trial, especially when there was no guarantee that they'd win without the thumbprint evidence. And they knew that the memories of some witnesses were fading five years after the fact.

So they struck a deal. On July 5, 1983, in a closed Duluth courtroom, Roger pleaded guilty to two counts of second-degree murder, a lesser charge than his original first-degree murder convictions. In return, he was allowed to go free, having served just over five years in prison. He gave a rambling and vague description of the murder, saying he was drunk at the time and didn't remember some of the crucial details.

At first glance, it doesn't seem like much of a deal from the prosecution's side. Roger confessed to two brutal murders, then was allowed to get out of jail — free. It was a classic example of plea bargaining, with all its advantages and disadvantages.

Technically, the murders were now solved, without the risk and expense of another trial. Still, many wondered at the wisdom of the deal and where justice could be found in this corner of the justice system.

Back in Latrobe, Caldwell's family still refused to believe he'd been involved in the murders. "He had to plead guilty to get out of jail," one said. "He would have been crazy not to."

Just a week after his release, Roger seemed mystified with the system: "If I did it, I should still be in jail. If I didn't do it, why did they spend all those years going after me?"

Roger decided to stay in Latrobe after making the deal, even though the entire town had found out about his troubles with the law. (Until Caldwell's release from prison, there had been no mention of the murders or Roger's trial in the Latrobe media. But then a Twin Cities reporter – not me – tipped off the Latrobe newspaper about Roger and it became front-page news.)

Roger was unable to find a job in Latrobe and went on welfare. At times, he filled in as a bartender at a local pub, which, he admitted, was not the best career choice for a recovering alcoholic.

Marjorie, meanwhile, continued to make news.

She married Wallace Hagen, a retired electrician and old family friend, in a 1981 North Dakota ceremony. Apparently, though, she forgot to divorce Roger first. Although she would claim that she obtained a quickie divorce in Mexico, no evidence of that divorce has ever emerged. North Dakota officials filed bigamy charges against her in March, 1983, but the crime didn't warrant extradition, so as long as she doesn't return to that state, it's unlikely she'll ever face trial.

When I learned about Marjorie's new marriage, I called Latrobe to see where and when Roger had been divorced. The word from Latrobe was that Roger had no knowledge of a divorce and was surprised and hurt that Marjorie had remarried. He probably shouldn't have been surprised. Marjorie had visited him in prison just once after her acquittal and had made no effort to contact him when he got out. Still, he maintained a loyalty to her, perhaps thinking that she'd take care of him, somehow, for all his efforts.

Trouble followed Marjorie after her wedding, too. She and Wally Hagen bought a house in Mound, a western Twin Cities suburb, in 1982, but when they couldn't come up with the money to pay off a contract for deed, they arranged to sell the house to another couple. But the house burned down mysteriously before the new owners could move in. Early in 1983 she was charged with arson and insurance fraud for burning down the house.

Meshbesher defended her again, but he couldn't work his magic this time. The jury found her guilty and Hennepin County District Judge Robert Schiefelbein sentenced her to 2½ years in prison and a $10,000 fine.

The day before she was sentenced, Marjorie was arrested in St. Louis Park for shoplifting a $7.99 bottle of vitamins from an upscale grocery store.

In January 1985, all her appeals ran out and she began serving her arson sentence at the Shakopee Women's Prison. She was released on parole in October 1986 and spent the winter in Arizona with Wally Hagen. Like many Minnesota snowbirds, she spent the next several years living in Arizona during the winter and returning to Minnesota in the summer.

The Aftermath

By his own account, Roger spent six miserable years in Latrobe following his release from prison. He was broke and became increasingly bitter as he failed to adjust to life on the outside.

At first, he seemed confident that he could overcome the stigma of the murder convictions. I visited him in 1983, just days after his plea bargain, and found him hopeful and energetic. He wanted to find work and put the prison days behind him. He hadn't heard from Marjorie in years, but suspected – and secretly hoped – that her lawyers might work out some sort of lucrative divorce deal, so he'd collect some of the Congdon money, after all.

It never happened. Caldwell went on welfare, getting $186 per month. He shared a small apartment near the old railway depot with a woman friend, for companionship and to save money. They survived with food stamps and clothes from the Salvation Army. Roger grew vegetables in the cramped back yard and regularly visited his mother and father in a nearby high-rise. He rarely saw his brothers, two of whom still lived in Latrobe, except at family gatherings.

Roger tended bar occasionally, but he realized it was a poor choice for an alcoholic and he also worried that the welfare people would find out and dock his welfare check. After a while, the effort of looking for a better job was too much, and he gave up.

In 1987 I visited Roger again. It was 10 years after the murders and he'd been out of prison for nearly five years. This time, Roger was morose and disheartened. He still had no job, no money and no prospects. He was driving a 14-year-old station wagon owned by his parents.

For the first time, though, he began to talk about the murders. Until then, he'd always refused to answer even simple questions, fearing that he'd be charged with perjury if he deviated in the least from the sworn confession he'd given in Duluth in return for his freedom.

But now, years later, he opened up a bit. There was a sense of doom in his works and in his manner. It was hard to tell if he didn't care any more or if he was talking to cleanse himself, to rid himself of some demons. Probably, it was some of each.

He said he hadn't committed the murders. He said he'd confessed only to get out of prison. "I was the patsy," he said. "An extremely wealthy person was murdered. Someone had to pay. My wife was the most hated person in the family and the only way to get to her was through me."

He said he'd been home – in the Colorado hotel room – on the night of the murders. He sounded sincere, but he couldn't explain the evidence that had convicted him in Brainerd. He said he was framed, although he couldn't say by whom. Then he didn't want to talk about it anymore.

It became clear that he was losing his will to live. As we drove together through the western Pennsylvania hills, he made several foreboding remarks.

"I'm so disenchanted with the hand I've been dealt, but there's not a thing I can do about it."

"You reach a point in your life when you just give up. The older you get, the more bleak it becomes. When you're young, you haven't been kicked in the head enough to give up. But when you reach a certain age, you realize there's nothing out there. You're glad you've got a television and a little yard to putter in." (He was 53 at the time.)

"I'm sick. I'm probably dying. I'll be surprised if I'm here next year. I'll be downright amazed if I'm here next year."

Eleven months later, on May 15, 1988, Roger Caldwell killed himself. He cut his wrists with a steak knife in the kitchen of his little apartment. Relatives said he'd been drinking heavily in the previous two weeks.

Earlier in the week he'd told relatives that he was terminally ill, but a check with his doctor proved that was untrue.

In his apartment, police found a note: "What you need to know is that I didn't kill those girls, or, to my knowledge ever harm a soul in my life."

But that wasn't true. He'd beaten his girlfriend just days before the suicide, sending her to the hospital. Those close to the case believe Roger was psychologically unable to admit, perhaps even to himself, that he'd killed Miss Congdon and Velma Pietila, the nurse. He tried, to the end, to blot out that memory from his mind. Alcohol was one of the tools he used.

Five days after his death, there was a service for Roger in the chapel of the Latrobe funeral home. Only nine people showed up to pay their last respects. Eight were relatives, and they graciously allowed me to sit in on the service. It rained all that day in Latrobe, and continued into the night.

～

The Mayhem
Continues

I n the late 1980s, Marjorie and Wally Hagen moved into the tiny retirement
community of Ajo, Arizona, pop. 3,500. It's about 80 miles south of Phoenix on
Hwy. 85. Chester Congdon had helped develop the copper mine that dominated the
small town for years. When the mine closed in the mid-1980s, many northerners
bought some of the tiny houses that previously had been rented to mine workers.
The houses were cheaper than most trailers, and provided an inexpensive way to
make an annual winter trek to Arizona.

Marjorie and Wally bought one of those little four-room houses. Wally's health
was poor – he was 82 now and had cancer, they said. Marjorie pushed him around
town in a wheelchair, stopping regularly to chat with neighbors.

Ajo, though, had a problem. A spate of arson fires plagued the town in late 1990
and early 1991. The burned homes had been empty, either abandoned or owned by
snowbirds who had already returned back north. Officials suspected a gang of youths
were responsible for the fires, but couldn't catch anyone.

Then, on March 24, 1991, a neighbor who lived two doors down from the
Hagens heard someone outside his window. He was a border patrol officer and wasn't
concerned when he saw Marjorie outside on the lawn, walking Wulf, the Hagens'
large dog. But something nagged at him and when he went outside to check, he
found a kerosene-soaked rag on his window.

He called the sheriff's office and when a team of deputies arrived they staked out
the area.

About 2 a.m. they heard someone approach. Then, they thought they heard a
match strike. They rushed out, extinguished the burning rag and chased the
perpetrator into the alley. It was Marjorie. They searched her for weapons, but not
for matches. Marjorie would later claim that she must be innocent because they
never found any matches on her. But she was charged with two counts of arson and
was a suspect in 13 other suspicious fires.

Wally couldn't raise the $50,000 bond to free Marjorie from jail. "All I have is
my Social Security," he said. "All the rest is tied up in judgments. And Marge's kids
won't help – they say she's gotten into trouble too many times before. I think that's
terrible, don't you?"

Wally said his wife was set up. He pointed to Wulf and said: "There's the culprit. I think someone put meat juice on the rag and Wulf took it off the windowsill. She was just returning it." It's the same argument she'd use at the trial, and beyond.

He said he didn't know why anyone would want to frame his wife.

"I'm standing by my wife," he said. "To my mind, she's innocent. I suppose you think it's strange I don't seem more upset. I suppose I should be, but things have always worked out in my life. I think this will, too." He didn't know it, but a year later, that would no longer be true.

This wasn't the Hagens' first run-in with Arizona authorities. They'd had a motor home repossessed, along with some of Marjorie's jewelry after a check for $55,000 bounced. They used the check to pay for major repairs to their large RV. And one of the Ajo fires had destroyed a warehouse where they kept another big RV. Marjorie later admitted setting that fire, saying she needed the insurance money to pay for Wally's medical care.

The Arizona Arson Trial

Marjorie stayed in jail for several months until Wally came up with the bail money. While Marjorie was "away," neighbors noticed a remarkable improvement in Wally's health. They said he didn't need his wheelchair anymore and was flirting with waitresses. And he started eating at his favorite restaurant, the local Kentucky Fried Chicken. When Marjorie was around, she wouldn't let him eat there.

When she finally was released, her lawyer successfully delayed the arson trial for more than a year, saying Wally was ill and needed his wife's attention.

The trial began in October 1992. Marjorie's lawyer stuck to her "Wulf" defense and argued that they'd never found a match on her that night. And Wally was called as one of the defense witnesses. In theatrical fashion so typical of Marjorie, Wally was wheeled into the courtroom on a gurney while the judge, jury and spectators watched in amazement. He gave his testimony lying down, with Wulf, who was described as a "hearing ear dog," at his side. Unfortunately for Marjorie's case, jurors watching out the window had seen Wally getting out of the car in front of the courthouse, unaided, and noticed Marjorie help him get up into the gurney.

Wally told the jury that Marjorie had trouble gripping items in her hands and was not able to light a match. Marjorie testified, too, that she was out walking the dog when she saw sparks near the neighbor's house. She said she became frightened and ran. She, too, said she was incapable of lighting a paper match, even though police had found a book of matches in her house.

The jurors were also told of Marjorie's Minnesota arson conviction. They were impressed with the weight of evidence against her and unimpressed with her flamboyant style. They convicted her of attempted arson on October 30. Because of her previous arson conviction she faced a mandatory prison sentence.

Under Arizona law, she was supposed to go directly to jail to await final sentencing and any appeals. But Marjorie turned on her charm. She told the judge that Wally couldn't survive on his own and if she was going to prison she had to find someone to watch over him. She pleaded for just 24 hours of freedom, to take care of Wally.

The judge gave her one more day.

The Death
of Wally

When Marjorie and Wally returned to Ajo, the local authorities were ready. Worried that Marjorie might make a break for Mexico, they kept an overnight watch on the house.

The next day, a sheriff's deputy smelled gas near the house. Tom Taylor, the lieutenant in the Pima County Sheriff's office overseeing the case, rushed over and knocked on the door of the little house at 721 Palo Verde Road. Marjorie came to a window and told Taylor that she'd accidentally left the gas oven on earlier, but that it was off now and that everything was okay.

She also said she planned to live up to her promise to turn herself in that afternoon, in just a few hours.

Taylor went back to his office, but a couple hours later he got a call from the Twin Cities. It was Tom Hagen, one of Wally's three children from his first marriage, saying Marjorie had just called him to say Wally was dead.

Taylor and a team of officers rushed back to the Palo Verde house and found Wally's body. At first Marjorie said she didn't know when Wally had died. Police searched the house, questioned her, then arrested her at 3:30 a.m. She was transferred to a jail in Tucson and charged with murder. Bail was set at $1 million.

Relatives reported that Marjorie had called one of her daughters from jail and said that Wally had died about noon, an hour before Taylor had questioned Marjorie about the gas smell.

"I hope they make this stick. I hope they put her away and throw away the key," said Jennifer Johnson, Marjorie's normally mild-mannered sister. The two sisters had not seen each other in years and Jennifer still held Marjorie responsible for their mother's death. Jennifer said she was shocked, but not surprised, at this latest turn of events.

Police found two suicide notes in the house, indicating that Wally may have believed he was entering into a suicide pact with Marjorie. But officials said they didn't think Marjorie ever had any intention of killing herself. A garden hose was found in the house, freshly cut, and apparently had been used to funnel gas into the bedroom.

The suicide notes, though, complicated the case. Prosecutors knew it would be difficult to prove beyond a reasonable doubt that Marjorie had been involved in

Wally's death. Three weeks after Wally's death, Arizona officials announced that they were temporarily dropping the murder charges.

They explained that, under Arizona law, a grand jury must be convened or a preliminary hearing held soon after charges are filed. But many of the tests on Wally's body and other forensic evidence tests were not ready yet, so prosecutors could not present their case in time to satisfy the legal requirements. Because Marjorie was already in jail on the attempted arson case, there was no sense of urgency.

Autopsy results in the case proved very interesting. Wally's body showed no signs of cancer, even though Marjorie had been claiming for years that he was dying of cancer. In fact, they first decided to move to Ajo after passing through on their way to Mexico to buy cancer drugs for Wally. They continued to make trips across the border to buy medication that is not available in the U.S., because it does not have FDA approval. And Marjorie often was seen injecting substances into Wally. Some of Wally's relatives said they suspected for years that Marjorie was exaggerating his illness and using drugs to keep him passive.

The official cause of death was determined to be an overdose of prescription pain medicine. The prescription was in Wally's name.

In May 1993, Marjorie was in prison when she pleaded no contest to another charge that she set two earlier fires at an Ajo repair shop, burning a car, a dump truck, a paint shed and two motor homes. One of the motor homes, valued at $35,000, belonged to the Hagens. Marjorie later admitted setting that fire in order to collect the insurance payment. She needed the money, she said, to pay Wally's medical bills.

Finally, in June, nearly eight months after her conviction, Marjorie was sentenced for the kerosene rag fire and the Ajo repair shop case. The judge gave her the maximum – 15 years. Her earliest possible release would be in 10 years, in 2002. The sentence was decreed by Judge Frank Dawley, the same judge who's presided over the trial and released her for a day after the conviction so she could take care of Wally. He also ordered her to pay $39,000 in restitution to the damaged repair shop.

The same day, officials said they would not charge Marjorie a second time for Wally's murder. They reasoned that Marjorie already had a hefty prison term ahead of her and they hoped to avoid the expense of a difficult trial. Marjorie was 59 at the time.

Taylor, the cop who'd pursued Marjorie on the arson cases and found Wally's body, had mixed feelings.

"I feel good that she got the maximum sentence on the arson charges, but I'm disappointed we couldn't make more progress on the murder charges," he said. "I would have liked to have had a jury look at all the facts."

Wally Hagen's children were also upset. In a letter to Judge Dawley, two of the children wrote: "She's a career criminal and must be put away for the protection of society in general, and us specifically."

Marjorie Hagen's
Arizona prison
mug shot.

Marjorie Hagen at her November, 2001 parole hearing at the Arizona State Prison in Parryville. Directly behind her is Tom Hagen, son of Wally Hagen. At the far left is Nancy Kaufmann, Wally's daughter.

The Parole Hearing

E ven though her arson sentence actually extended until February 2007, Marjorie Hagen's first chance at parole in Arizona came up Nov. 15, 2001. In the weeks before the hearing, a flurry of letters arrived in Phoenix urging the parole board to keep her locked up.

With Wally dead, Marjorie really had only one active supporter: her lawyer, Ed Bolding. He was a long-time friend and had represented her through all the troubles.

Bolding called her a misunderstood grandmother who had been in prison far too long for attempted arson and said she should be released on parole.

"She's done well in prison, she's not a danger to the community, and she's been an outstanding teacher in the prison system," Bolding said. The 15-year sentence was way too harsh for attempted arson, he said. "I've had clients serve less time for murder," he said.

But Jennifer Johnson and Wally's children disagreed passionately. Their letters to the parole board were stamped "Opposed."

"We just don't want her out," Jennifer said.

Wrote Nancy Kaufmann, one of Wally's three children: "One of our concerns is that she'll get out and fleece some other poor soul. I'd hate to see some other gentleman get taken in like my dad."

Jennifer Johnson, too, said she's worried that her sister "could latch onto another family and ruin their lives" when released. "I just can't get beyond it, not after what she did to my mother. The hurt never goes away." In her letter, Jennifer called Marjorie "the mastermind behind her husband, Roger Caldwell, in killing our mother."

Bolding read all the letters in advance of the hearing and noted that they were "dripping with vitriol." But he said he understands the Hagen children's grief. "They believe Ms. Hagen was instrumental in the death of their father; she was charged with that, but it was rightly dismissed."

Research prior to the hearing showed that during her years in the Arizona prison system, Marjorie had been found guilty of 12 prison violations, including lying to officials, disobeying orders and refusing to work. In her 2001 prison profile, though, she was not considered a public or institutional risk. Her prison jobs over the years included law library clerk, education aide, yard worker and chaplain clerk.

The day before the parole hearing, two of Wally's children, Nancy Kaufmann and Tom Hagen, flew to Phoenix. "I want her to know that I'm still watching her," Nancy said.

At the hearing, Marjorie wore a bright orange prison suit, with her gray hair pulled back in a bun. She sat in a plastic chair inside a cinder block classroom inside the San Pedro Unit of Arizona's Perryville Prison. Seeing the Hagens in the room, she launched into a complaint about how Wally's family wouldn't help pay for his medical care and had turned against their father in his time of need. She even implied that the children had neglected their mother. This really irked the Hagens, who have always suspected that Marjorie had a role in their mother's death, too, because Marjorie was the last one to visit her at a nursing home before Helen died unexpectedly.

Parole members wondered why Marjorie had launched this personal attack in her bid for freedom. To get her back on track, they asked if she was guilty and remorseful.

"I burned the RV to take the insurance money to pay medical bills for Wally," she said. "I was frantic because the children wouldn't help pay."

But she wouldn't take responsibility for the kerosene rag at her neighbor's house. The deputy who lived there never liked her dog, she claimed. And all she'd done was put what she thought was an old jacket up on the window. And, she said, if she had tried to light it, why didn't the police find a match or a lighter at the scene?

A board member asked what she planned to do when released. She said she planned to move into a mobile home park near Tucson and volunteer at churches. She said she'd been meeting with psychologists to deal with her anger. She even took a class in prison called "Women Who Love Too Much."

This was all too much for Tom Hagen. He told the board: "You've heard a lot of lies today." He called Marjorie a habitual liar and said his parents were always well cared for.

"If you let this woman out, it's only a matter of time before she'll start another fire," he said. "Starting fires is her tool for anger management. She's not just a grandmother, she's an arsonist."

A parole board member asked Marjorie why none of her children were advocating for her release. (One daughter had even written to the board, asking for denial of parole.)

Marjorie replied: "I attribute that to our fight over money."

In the end, the board said no. Not this time.

The Release

But they couldn't keep her locked up forever, and on Jan. 5, 2004, Marjorie's time was up.

She was 71 and had spent nearly 11 years in the Arizona prison system. (Her 15-year sentence was scheduled to run until 2007, but she earned the early release date under new Arizona state rules designed to ease prison overcrowding.)

There was much worry about the release. Marjorie's sister, Jennifer Johnson, issued a warning: "I'm worried there'll be more trouble," she said. "I can't believe she'll stay quiet; it's not like her. I'm worried she'll do something awful, again."

The Hagen family, too, had concerns.

"We're very frustrated that there's never been any satisfaction for us in the death of our dad, and probably our mother," Nancy Kaufmann said. "People ask if I fear for my life now that Marjorie's getting out. In some respects, I wish she'd come after me and get caught. I feel so sorry for any unsuspecting men out there who she tries to get her hooks into."

But there was nothing they could do.

About 10 a.m. on a sunny Arizona Monday, a rented car pulled up to the prison and Marjorie, carrying a box of her belongings, climbed inside. A television news crew tried to follow, but the car sped away.

She is free to live anywhere she wants and is not subject to unannounced visits by parole officers. But Ajo residents said they hope she doesn't return to their quiet town.

Many suspected it wouldn't be long, though, before we'd hear from Marjorie again. And it wasn't. On March 30, 2007- at age 74- she was charged with fraud and forgery in Tucson.

Prosecutors alleged that she befriended an elderly man with a heart problem in an assisted living facility and convinced him to sign a power of attorney agreement. When he died March 1, 2007, she told officials that he had no relatives and arranged for a hasty cremation. No autopsy was conducted.

Bank officials became suspicious when Marjorie allegedly forged the dead man's name on a check and deposited the money in her own account.

The Tour

Welcome to Glensheen.

The guides – they like to be called docents – escort 80,000 people through the mansion each year, proudly showing off this historic 39-room home on the shores of Lake Superior in Duluth.

During the official tour, the guides, dressed in 1910-era clothing, will point out the architectural highlights of the mansion, the hand-carved woodwork, the gold leaf ceilings, the 15 bedrooms, 15 fireplaces and eight bathrooms

They'll also describe, in great detail, the outstanding furnishings found throughout the house.

"The light fixture in the reception room is carved alabaster. And the coffee table is made of in-laid marble."

"The silver lamps above the fireplace in the library came from the Egypt."

But when it comes to the murders, the guides are very circumspect. For more than 20 ears they were told not to even mention the homicides, and to ward off any questions about which bedroom was Miss Congdon's or where the killer washed up after the murders.

The following pages will help you incorporate the story of the infamous Congdon Murder case into the official tour of Glensheen. You'll know exactly who, what, where, when and how.

The University of Minnesota now owns the mansion; Miss Congdon transferred the title before her death. For years, the university abided by the Congdon family's wishes to downplay the murders. They worried that talk of the tragedy would diminish the family's legacy. As time passes and the questions continue, officials recognize that the murders have become part of the mansion's mystique.

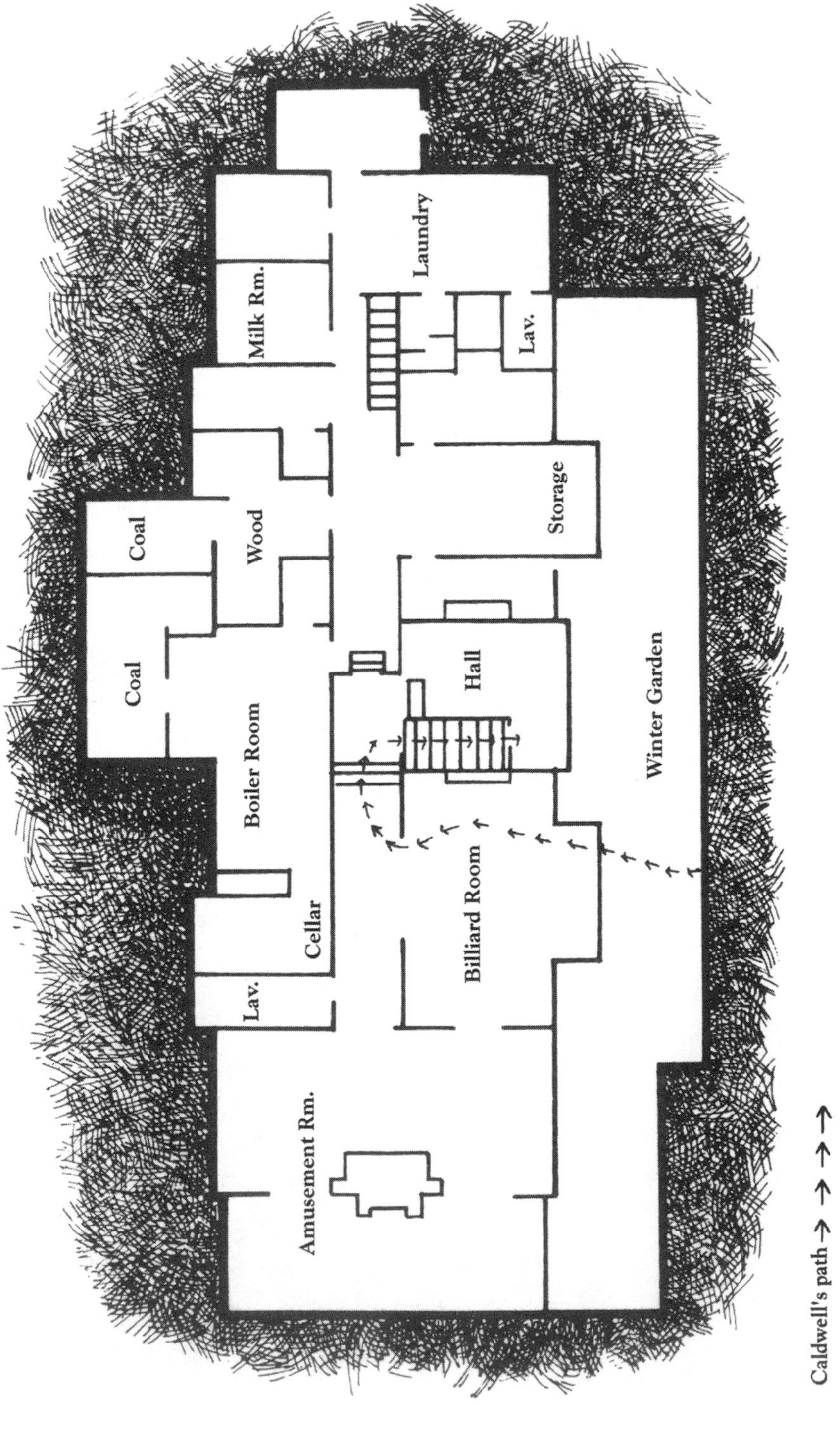

Ground Floor Plan

Caldwell's path → → →

Amusement Rm.

Lav.

Cellar

Boiler Room

Coal

Coal

Wood

Milk Rm.

Billiard Room

Hall

Winter Garden

Storage

Lav.

Laundry

The Ground Floor

Although an interesting part of the tour, the bottom floor of Glensheen contains just a few items pertaining to the murders. (Unlike regular houses, the mansion doesn't seem to have a basement, for the guides always refer to it as the lower level or the ground floor.)

As a child, Marjorie played in all the rooms down here, in the laundry room and the milk room and the boiler room. But, of course, the servants did all the work in those areas.

But in the billiard room, take notice of the windows looking out toward the lake. Through those windows, and from the windows in the amusement room next door, you can see the patio area, or the subway, as the Congdon family called it.

On the night of the murders, the exterior windows had been removed from this area so Caldwell was able to walk right into the subway. From there, he broke a window in the rear alcove of the billiard room. He said in his confession that he didn't remember what he used to break the window, but police believe it was a rock or tool he found nearby.

Caldwell then reached through the broken window, unlocked it, pulled it open and climbed through. Broken glass was found on the floor. Then he made his way around the ancient billiard table and into the long hallway, where he began climbing the stairs towards Miss Congdon's bedroom.

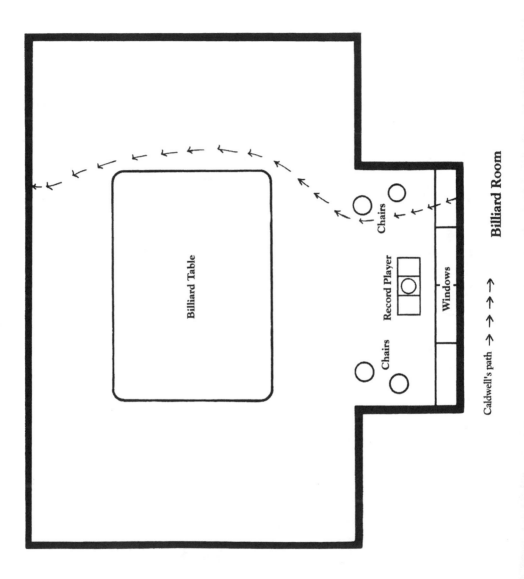

Billiard Room

Caldwell's path → → →

The
Billiard Room

Roger Caldwell entered the mansion by breaking one of the windows in the billiard room – one of the middle windows in the room's rear alcove. He smashed a small hole in the window with a heavy object, scattering glass more than 16 feet across the room.

During Roger's trial, there was much discussion about the size of the hole in the window compared to the size of Roger's biceps, and whether he could have reached into the hole and opened the latch.

Police found a 6-by-4 inch hole in the double locked window. During the investigation, five Duluth policemen tried to reach through the hole to undo the locks and open the window. Only one officer, Barry Brooks, was successful.

Police measured Roger's arms and found his biceps and forearms were less than half-an-inch larger than Brooks' biceps and forearms. Police and prosecutors were satisfied that Roger's arms would have fit.

But defense attorney Doug Thomson was not satisfied. He created a cardboard replica of the window, with the middle cut out to represent the hole, complete with cardboard made to look like shards of glass. During Roger's trial, he faced Officer Brooks on the witness stand and asked Brooks to reach through the simulated hole.

Halfway through, Brooks' arm caught on a cardboard shard. He wiggled his arm the rest of the way through the hole. "So your arm doesn't fit?" Thomson asked. "Well, I made it through," Brooks replied.

In his confession, Roger said simply that he "reached all the way through" the window and unlocked it.

"I remember walking past a pool table and getting to the stairs and my intention was to get up to Miss Congdon's bedroom," he said.

The billiard table, by the way, has been in that room since 1909.

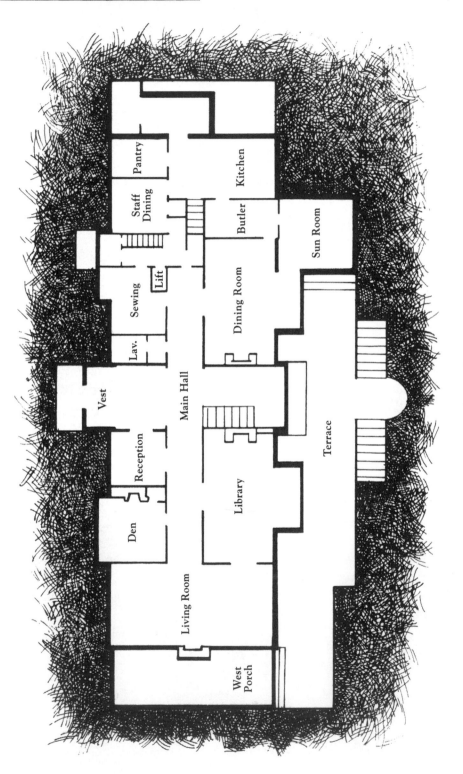

First Floor Plan

The
First Floor

As you move upstairs on the tour, from the ground floor to the first floor, you will follow Roger's footsteps.

He carried no flashlight that night, so imagine him inching his way upward, feeling his way along the wall in the dark. When he reached the main floor, he continued up the stairs.

The official tour, though, branches off to examine the rest of the main floor, before continuing upstairs.

The library, with its large marble fireplace and Angora goat's wool wallcovering, is where Roger met with Miss Elisabeth on his visit to the mansion, one month before the murders.

The two, the family matriarch and her new son-in-law, chatted for about half an hour in the library. He brought her a tiny Chinese carved horse, a gift from Marjorie. He also told her about Colorado.

Roger had come to Duluth, without Marjorie, to ask the trustees of the Congdon estate for money, claiming that he and his wife needed to buy a Colorado ranch because Ricky – Marjorie's youngest son and Elisabeth's grandson – had asthma and needed to live in the mountains. But on that day Roger did not discuss finances with his mother-in-law. He'd been well prepared and knew that she no longer held the purse strings and that to discuss money might create problems, giving Marjorie's history of overspending.

In a meeting later that day with the trustees, Roger's request was denied.

Except for the front door and hallway, Roger never saw the rest of the mansion's main floor that day. But on the night of the murders, Roger raced down the stairway after killing the two women. He was quite drunk and probably didn't even notice the ornamental glass or the floor-to-ceiling oak paneling or the Oriental rugs in the hallway.

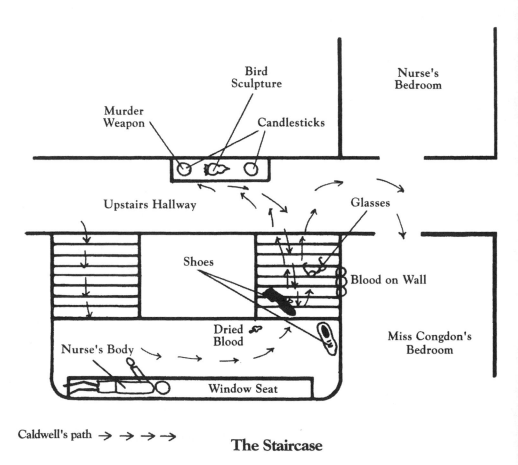

Bird Sculpture

Murder Weapon

Candlesticks

Nurse's Bedroom

Upstairs Hallway

Glasses

Shoes

Blood on Wall

Dried Blood

Miss Congdon's Bedroom

Nurse's Body

Window Seat

Caldwell's path → → → →

The Staircase

The Staircase

As Roger Caldwell inched his way up the stairway that night in the darkness, passing from the main floor to the second floor, he was startled by a sound from above. A door opened at the top of the stairs and the night nurse, Velma Pietila, appeared with a flashlight.

As she started down the steps, Roger rushed toward her. They struggled for a moment near the top of the stairs, but Roger was stronger and had the element of surprise. He knocked the 65-year-old woman to the mid-level landing below. Roger took a brass candlestick holder – the left one from a set of two on a table at the stairtop – and went down to the nurse. He hit her repeatedly.

They struggled again. With her last reserves of strength she clawed at his head, pulling out pieces of hair. Blood spattered on the wall, halfway between the top and the landing. Pools of blood collected on the landing.

Pietila's flashlight, now broken, lay near the top of the steps. Her shoes were off; one lay partway up the stairs, the other on the landing. Her glasses were found on the stairs, not far from her body.

When the relief nurse arrived at 7 a.m. the next morning, she found Pietila's body on the landing, lying on the window seat overlooking the mansion grounds and Lake Superior.

The relief nurse's first thought – seeing her friend lying there – was, Why is Velma taking a nap? It took a moment before the terrifying truth sunk in.

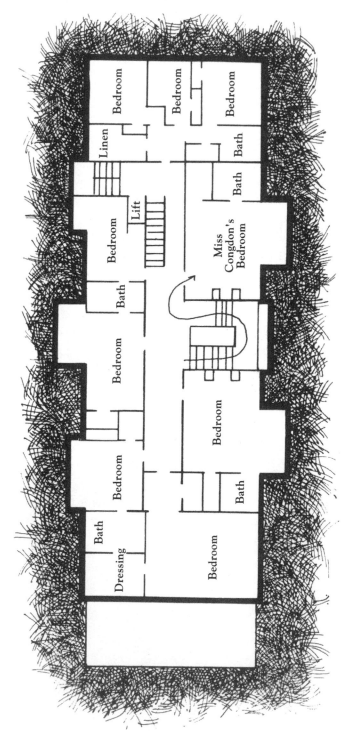

Second Floor Plan

Caldwell's path → → → →

The
Second Floor

As you continue the tour on the second floor, you'll find an impressive array of bedrooms, with their distinctive fireplaces and unique furnishings.

But for years, no one would tell you which bedroom was Elisabeth Congdon's. Well, here's where it is.

When you climb the main stairway up to the second floor, it's the first bedroom around to the right, with windows looking out on the lake.

For a time after the murders, Miss Congdon's bedroom was used as a meeting room, lined with dozens of chairs. In 1983, though, it once again was restored as a bedroom.

Just across the hall from Miss Congdon's room is a small bathroom where the killer washed up after the murders. Blood was found spattered in the bathroom and police found a mysterious fingerprint on the sink. It was definitely not Roger's fingerprint, the experts agreed. For a while the print was known as the "mystery print" and the defense attorneys were salivating of using it to convince the jury that the real killer was still on the loose. But further investigation showed that the print belonged to Police Sgt. Gary Waller, chief investigator on the case who went on to a fine career as the St. Louis County Sheriff.

There are servant's quarters on the second floor of the mansion, separated from the main bedrooms by a heavy door. A cook was sleeping there on the night of the murders and was awakened about 2:45 a.m. when her black poodle, "Muffin," began barking.

The cook took the dog with her when she went to the bathroom. On the way back to her room, the dog leapt from her arms and ran up to the heavy door separating the two sections. The cook did not open the door, but brought the dog back to her room. Muffin kept whining until 5 a.m.

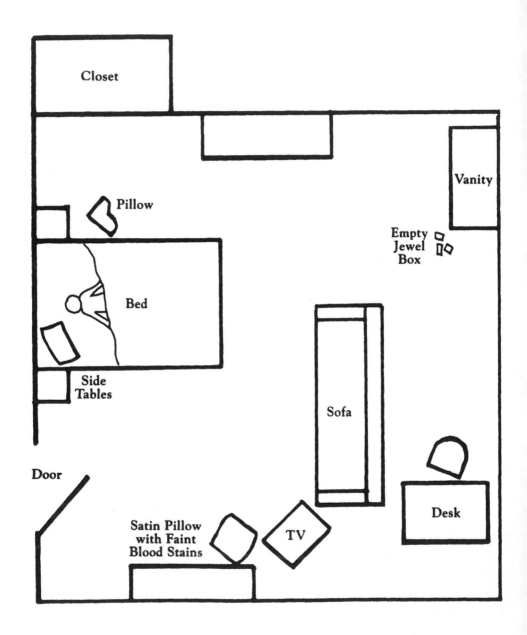

Closet

Pillow

Vanity

Empty
Jewel
Box

Bed

Side
Tables

Sofa

Desk

Door

Satin Pillow
with Faint
Blood Stains

TV

Miss Congdon's Bedroom

The Victim's Bedroom

Elisabeth Congdon went to sleep about 10:50 p.m. on Sunday night, June 26, 1977. She had just returned from a weekend outing at the family's Brule River cabin in Wisconsin. She was tired but very happy, according to an attendant.

Her bed that night was just to the left of the door. A davenport, desk, television, chest of drawers and vanity filled the rest of the room.

The killer entered the room long after she'd first fallen asleep. It's likely that she heard the commotion as the killer and her nurse battled on the stairway, not far from her room. But she was immobilized by her stroke and unable to flee.

The killer pulled a satin pillow from beneath her head and held it firmly over her face. She tried to escape, but couldn't.

When she stopped moving, the killer searched through her vanity and chest of drawers, looking for jewelry. He found a small wicker basket in the closet and filled it with the chosen jewelry. Then he took a watch and ring from Miss Congdon's hand and wrist, and added them to the collection in the basket.

He found a gold Byzantine coin in a memorabilia box on the desk and took it, too.

He left the room to wash up in the bathroom across the hall. He found the nurse's keys in the adjoining bedroom, then hurried down the stairs, past the dead nurse's body, and out the front door.

He found the nurse's car parked nearby and drove it to the Minneapolis/St. Paul International Airport.

The next morning, police responding to an emergency call made by the cook and nurse, found the satin pillow with faint bloodstains lying on Miss Congdon's bedroom floor near the fireplace. Empty jewelry boxes were scattered by the vanity, in the corner diagonally opposite the doorway.

Miss Congdon, 83-years-old, was in her bed, dead.

∼

Roger Caldwell, at home in Latrobe in 1987, 10 years after the murders. He tended a small garden behind his apartment.

Caldwell stood in front of his Latrobe apartment, which was above a bar.

Roger Caldwell inside his Latrobe apartment.

The Inside Stories

I t was a bit of luck and good timing that led me to the Congdon murder case. I was scheduled to write a routine newspaper story about strawberries that June day in 1977 but stumbled instead on what would become Minnesota's Crime of the Century.

Back then I was a rookie reporter for the Minneapolis Tribune, writing stories for the Sunday Farm and Home section. I got an early start that Monday morning and headed north on the freeway to interview the strawberry farmers near Askov, Minn., on the way to Duluth.

The car didn't have an FM radio, so I listened to WCCO-AM, and about 45 minutes into the two-hour drive, a news bulletin flashed on the radio saying police in the Duluth had found the bodies of two women, apparent victims of homicide. Details were still very sketchy.

I was an eager young reporter, much more interested in covering crime news than strawberries, so this opportunity was too good to ignore. I pulled off the freeway, found a pay phone and called the newspaper office. The only editor on duty said she hadn't heard about any murders in Duluth.

It's all over the radio and I'm halfway there, so why don't I just keep driving and check it out? I suggested.

Sure. Why not? She radioed ahead to the photographer, who was scheduled to meet me at the strawberry farm and sent her along to Duluth, too. The editor didn't seem hopeful that it would amount to much and later we would joke that if she'd realized what a big story this was going to be, she would have immediately sent a real reporter to cover it.

So I happily drove back onto the freeway and headed north.

Later radio reports said that the murder scene was on London Road, but that meant nothing to me. Two of my uncles and their families lived in Duluth, but I had only been there a handful of times and didn't know many street names. So I drove downtown and found the police station. A sergeant at the front desk explained that London Road was the main road leading up toward the North Shore and pointed me in the right direction. But good luck getting close, he said, because the scene had been secured.

I soon found the address, guarded by a cluster of police cars. It was a mansion. I parked a couple blocks away and walked into a crowd that included several reporters and camera people standing outside an iron fence that defends the huge mansion.

In these situations, bystanders often like to show off their knowledge, and several in the crowd filled me in: the mansion belonged to Elisabeth Congdon, an elderly heiress from one of the city's leading families. She had been paralyzed years earlier by a stroke and needed around-the-clock nursing care; apparently she was now dead. The second victim was Miss Congdon's overnight nurse.

Police officers at the gate refused to answer questions. A press announcement would be released later in the day, they said.

Soon I found the photographer who'd been scheduled to shoot the strawberry farm. She'd been notified about the change of plans and was looking for a way to photograph the murder scene, but the late June growth of trees and bushes completely blocked all views of the mansion from the road.

Several curious youngsters were in the crowd on this summer morning, so I asked a young boy on a bike if he knew anyone with a boat. The boy, about 12, said he lived just a few blocks up the road and had a little fishing boat. We offered him $10 if we could borrow the boat for a few minutes.

We got permission from his mother and he took the photographer out on the lake. Their mission was a great success; she got a great shot of the lakeside of the mansion for the next day's paper.

Meanwhile, I used the family's phone to report in to the office. By now, the editors back in the office had figured out that this was a big story and had assigned some help. Two veteran reporters, Peg Meier and Neal Gendler, began working on the story from Minneapolis, getting lots of background on the Congdon family while I continued to get details from the scene.

According to the official police version, the women were killed when an intruder broke into the mansion, killed Miss Congdon and the nurse, then stole some items from the bedroom and fled in the nurse's car.

The car was found later in the day at the Twin Cities International Airport. In retrospect, the car at the airport was a major clue that this case was more complicated that a simply burglary gone awry. But we didn't pick up on it right away.

Late that night, when we finished the story for the Tuesday morning paper, the editors told me to get a hotel room so I could follow up the next day. They told me to buy some new clothes and a toothbrush.

~

Inside Stories: The Nurse

The next morning I returned to the police station to see if anything new had arisen overnight. It hadn't. But the editors wanted something new, so I wracked my brain.

Miss Congdon's daytime nurse, Mildred Garvue, had found the bodies when she reported to work at 7 a.m. Police officers had said she didn't want to talk to the media, but it seemed worth a chance. Her phone was busy for over an hour, so I drove to her house in a quiet, wooded area of Duluth. Her husband was out front, cutting the grass.

I introduced myself, but he said his wife wasn't home. Besides, she had already turned down interview requests from the Duluth newspaper and television stations, he said. Disappointed, I started to leave. But then we started to chat. It turned he was a high school athletic director and my uncle had been the school's choir director. His Duluth basketball team had been in the state tournament a few years back; so had my team. We'd been talking for several minutes when a car pulled up. It was Nurse Garvue, home from the grocery store. Her husband called to her: "Honey, this is Joe Kimball from the Minneapolis paper. His uncle is the choir guy."

She smiled. I helped carry in the groceries and we spent the afternoon in her kitchen, talking about Miss Congdon and the murders. She offered me cake and introduced me to her daughter as we discussed the case. Until then, I knew very little about Miss Congdon, the person. Our sources had talked the day before about her philanthropy and her role as the youngest daughter of Chester Congdon, the lawyer who made a fortune in the Minnesota mining business, but not about her private life.

But Mildred talked about the real Elisabeth, saying she was a short but regal dowager who loved to listen to Chopin records as she moved slowly around the giant house. She told how Miss Congdon loved to play cards, even though her right side had been paralyzed by the stroke. A special wooden board had been made to hold the cards, so she could shuffle and play one-handed. Even the stroke didn't slow her down when it came to cards. She played a mean gin rummy.

Mildred told me about Miss Congdon's daily routine: She'd groom and exercise each morning, and lunch was always a big deal, served in the bedroom overlooking the lake. Afternoons, the staff would take her around the estate in a wheelchair.

Miss Congdon was a diabetic who needed daily insulin shots. She took a sedative most nights to help her sleep, but Mildred said none had been given on the night of the murder. She had checked the next morning.

This was all great information and I jotted everything down in my notebook. It was the first real glimpse into everyday life at the Congdon Mansion and I knew it would make a great story.

Then talk turned to the murders. Quietly and slowly, Mildred described the scene, how she'd gone first to the kitchen to get Miss Congdon's insulin, then started up the main stairs. She saw the body of her friend and fellow nurse, Velma Pietila, in the stairwell. She took her friend's pulse, then realized that Miss Congdon was upstairs, alone.

"I ran to her room. Right away I saw the pillow on her face. I didn't want to look but I had to. I could tell she was dead. I went back to Velma and then I saw two pools of blood."

This was hard for her to remember and to put into words, but I gently continued and asked about Miss Congdon's room. Mildred closed her eyes, remembering the scene, and described it to me. She talked about a bloodstained pillow tossed on the floor by the television; an empty jewelry box lay by the vanity. I was frantically taking notes, but I had trouble visualizing the room, so she took my notebook and drew a detailed map of the room, complete with bed, sofa, desk and closet.

Finally I left the house and called the editors from a pay phone. They were as excited as I was about the nurse's revelations and told me to start writing. Two problems remained. They wanted the sketch of Miss Congdon's bedroom for the next day's paper, but it was too late to drive it back to Minneapolis. They also wanted a photo of Nurse Garvue, but our photographer had returned the day before. It appeared the best bet to fulfill both requests was the Duluth newspaper.

I drove to the newspaper office and introduced myself to the local editors. I asked to use their transmitting machine, an early version of today's fax machine. Not wanting to let on what I had, I said there were some notes I needed to send back to Minneapolis. They agreed. I hovered over the machine during the transmission, so no one could see the pages. Then I told them that my editors were looking for a picture of Nurse Garvue, and wondered if they would send a photographer to shoot it. They said they'd already tried and been turned down. Without being specific, I said I'd had a chat with her and that she'd agreed to a picture. Besides, I told them, she'd likely be a witness at a trial someday and they'd be glad they had such a photo in their files. They were reluctant, but finally agreed that if a photographer were free later in the day, they'd do it.

I wrote my story and called it in, then waited two hours for the photographer. Finally one was cleared for the assignment and we went together to the Garvue home. It just took a minute or two, then we returned to the newspaper office where the photographer transmitted the photograph to the Associated Press, which in turn sent it to our Minneapolis office. The story was complete.

∾

Inside Stories:
Source Trouble

T he story, complete with bedroom sketch and photo of the nurse, ran on the front page of our paper the next day and it was a big scoop. Even the Duluth paper, which had a dozen reporters working on the story, had nowhere near the details we had of the murder scene and Miss Congdon's personal life. The details from Nurse Garvue helped readers understand that she wasn't some haughty heiress who'd been tragically killed, but a real person; a grandmother who was a gracious lady.

I check in at the police station, but Ernie Grams, the chief of detectives, said there was nothing new on the case. But then I got disturbing news from the newspaper office. Someone had called to say that Nurse Garvue, who had been so helpful in preparing the story about Miss Congdon and the crime scene, was illegally working in the mansion that day.

The report, which turned out to be true, said that Garvue's nursing license had been suspended six months earlier when she'd been caught signing out narcotics for her hospital patients, then taking them herself.

I was shocked and saddened to hear this. During our lengthy interview I hadn't asked about her nursing history and she hadn't volunteered anything about her past. Now the editors insisted that because we had based a major story on her eyewitness account, we must now tell the readers about her past. They planned another story about her drug problems and asked if I wanted to help write it.

At first I said no, arguing that we shouldn't even run such a story. Her situation was unfortunate, but she was not a suspect and therefore her previous problems had no bearing on the case. We didn't publish stories about other nurses who lost their licenses, I said.

But the editor was clear. There would be a story. And if I didn't want to call Mildred Garvue and get her side of the story, someone else would. So I did it. Mildred listened quietly as I nervously outlined the situation. Then she admitted the allegations, saying she'd been having trouble with arthritis and used the drugs to help ease the pain. She was not addicted, nor was she currently taking them, she said.

The Congdon family doctor knew about her drug problem and about the suspended license, but hired her anyway, she said. I said I was very sorry that her problems would be made so public, and warned her that after our paper ran the story, the Duluth newspaper and television stations likely would, too. I suggested that she find a place, out of town, to stay for a few days.

It was the low point of all my coverage of the story. Eight years later, when I published the first edition of this book, I appeared at a Duluth bookstore for a well-advertised book signing. The phone was ringing as I walked in. It was Mildred. She said she was mad at me. I was mortified and apologized anew for that old story about her drug problem.

"No, no. Not that," she said. "I'm mad that you didn't call me while you were writing your book. I have lots more information, and pictures, too, of Miss Congdon and all the nurses. You should have called."

As I signed books in Duluth that night, my heart was lighter, knowing Mildred had forgiven me.

Inside Stories:
The Duluth Sleuth

Those first few days in Duluth were heady and exciting, but much of the time I wasn't sure who to interview or where to look for new information. After the Mildred scoop/fiasco I settled into a routine that largely consisted of waiting in the police station for new leads.

Fortunately, I found a friend.

Ernie Grams, Duluth's chief of detectives, was in charge of the investigation. He had a team of officers working the case, led by Sgt. Gary Waller, but Ernie ran the show. In the waiting room, just outside his office, I set up an unofficial newspaper bureau. Each morning I'd check in with him, then go to the courthouse clerk to see if any search warrants or other documents had been filed. Then I'd use the nearby pay phone to call Congdon family members or business associates, and to check in with the main newsroom.

But I'd always return to Ernie's office, to chat with him as he'd come and go. He was always friendly, although not particularly forthcoming with new information. Early on he mentioned that before he became a police officer, he'd been a reporter for the Duluth newspaper.

"So, you feel sorry for me," I said.

"No, I just understand what it's like," he said.

Day by day, bits of information were revealed. The killer had stolen jewelry from Miss Congdon's room. (We already knew that, thanks to Mildred.) A search of the freeway between Duluth and the Minneapolis airport turned up nothing. (Police had hoped to find bloody clothing or other evidence that the killer might have thrown out while fleeing the mansion.) Police found blood in a mansion bathroom. (The killer tried to clean up after the bloody battle with Nurse Pietila.)

Six days after the murders, though, there was a breakthrough. While sitting in the police waiting room, I overheard two cops on the case talking about Denver, Colorado. It sounded like one officer was making arrangements to fly there. I wondered why he would be planning a vacation in the midst of this big murder case. But the more I heard the more I wondered if this trip was related to the murder. If so, it was quite a departure from the official version of the murders, which, police still publicly maintained, had been committed during a robbery.

Not sure what to do with the information, I called the Minneapolis editors and told them of my suspicions. Then I decided to bluff. That afternoon, I went into Ernie's office, closed the door and said: "I heard about Colorado."

"Where'd you hear that?" he asked.

"I hear things," I said.

He thought a minute, then said: "Okay. I'll make you a deal." He said he'd fill me in on the latest developments, if I promised not to print any of it until they'd made an arrest, and he gave me the go-ahead. They were still putting all the pieces together and he worried that the suspects might destroy evidence if they knew police were on to them.

I agreed to his arrangement and sat back to hear the story.

It turned out that within minutes of learning about the murders, Congdon family members had told police that they suspected two people: Marjorie, Miss Congdon's adopted daughter, and Roger Caldwell, Marjorie's second husband. The Caldwells lived in Colorado and were desperately short of cash, family members said. Just a month before, Roger had come to Duluth asking the family trustees for money and been turned down. They also told police about the time Miss Congdon become violently ill after eating some marmalade brought to her by Marjorie.

Grams said he was working with police in Colorado to gather evidence against the Caldwells; they'd already searched the couple's hotel room in Golden, Colorado, and Duluth detectives were keeping a close eye on them now that they'd returned to Minnesota for the funeral.

These were amazing revelations. It was the first anyone outside the family or police department had heard about the Marjorie connection, but I'd made a deal and felt I could trust Grams to fill me in when the time was right. The Fourth of July holiday had come, so I drove home from Duluth.

On July 5, I went into the Minneapolis newsroom and was hit with a bombshell. Earlier, when I had first mentioned a possible Colorado connection to the editors, they had sent reporter Peg Meier to Denver to poke around. That morning, she'd stumbled on a search warrant filed in the county courthouse. It outlined the complete case against the Caldwells, with even more information than Grams had given me.

"This is great," I told an editor. "But we really we can't run it yet. I promised Lt. Grams that we'd wait until he gave the word."

"That's nuts," the editor said. "First of all, we got all the information independently. Those are public records at a courthouse. Anyone could walk in there and find it. Second, reporters aren't authorized to make those kinds of deals. So don't do it again."

So again I had to make a painful phone call. I reached Grams and explained the situation, saying that we would have the story about the Caldwells in the next day's paper. Then I apologized. He was silent for a long moment, then said: "Now we'll have to lay all our cards on the table." Then he hung up.

We finished writing the story, which had the headline: "Son-in-law a suspect in Congdon Murders." When I got home, about 11:30 p.m., the phone rang. It was Grams, calling from Duluth.

"I promised to tell you when we made an arrest. Well, we picked up Roger Caldwell an hour ago," he said.

Even though I hadn't lived up to my end of the bargain, he had. He went on to give me the details of the arrest: Roger had been arrested at a hospital, where he was being treated for an apparent heart attack. (It turned out not to have been a heart attack.) Police found some of Miss Congdon's missing jewelry in the Caldwells' hotel room.

After he hung up, I called the newspaper office and we were able to change the top of the story. The headline was changed to: "Son-in-law arrested in Duluth slaying probe." It was another big scoop.

My respect for Grams was unbounded. I continued to speak with him as the investigation continued and once, during a lull in the case, wrote a long feature story about him. I called him the "Duluth Sleuth" and talked about his ever-present cigar and the gruff exterior that masked a warm human being.

The people of St. Louis County must have agreed with my assessment; they elected him sheriff in 1982. Four years later, on Sept. 22, 1986, Grams died in a car crash while driving home from work. He was 62.

Inside Stories:
The Lawyers

Soon after his arrest, Roger Caldwell hired St. Paul attorney Doug Thomson. The gray-haired lawyer was considered one of the top defense attorneys in the region. He'd been involved in the T. Eugene Thompson murder trial in the early 1960s, which, until the Congdon murders, had been considered one of the state's most sensational murders. (Thompson, a hotshot lawyer, was convicted of hiring a hit man to kill his wife. Doug Thomson defended Norman Mastrian, the middleman.) That was before my time, but I'd covered Thomson in other high-profile cases like June Mikulanec, who heard voices and stabbed her old boyfriend's new wife 98 times. And he defended Donald Larson in the Virginia Piper kidnapping case; Larson and Kenneth Callahan had been convicted of the kidnapping, but in a 1979 retrial, were acquitted. Thomson also defended Lois Jurgens, convicted in 1987 in the death of her adopted son, 22 years earlier.

Thomson began preparing the criminal case out of public view, meeting with Roger in the county jail. But one day I ran into another prominent Twin Cities lawyer in Duluth. Ron Meshbesher was doing research in the courthouse. I thought he might be helping Thomson with Roger's trial, but he said he was working for Marjorie Caldwell on the civil side -- the inheritance issues.

Soon after the murders, most of Marjorie's children from her first marriage had filed a civil lawsuit to keep her from getting any of Miss Congdon's money. The children argued that their mother had been involved in their grandmother's death. Marjorie needed a sharp lawyer to protect her interests, as forces began to mount from all sides.

In August, Marjorie appeared with a black eye and bruised face, claiming that a mysterious man had beaten her up while she was visiting one of her sons in Fridley. Police investigated and decided that her wounds were self-inflicted. Evidence of her craziness was mounting.

In September I ran into Meshbesher and Marjorie at the Hennepin County courthouse in Minneapolis, where they were doing research on their case. Marjorie proceeded to tell me she was being followed by someone, the police or private detectives, she thought. She said she'd even confronted them at a restaurant. It turned out that 10 Congdon family members had hired private detectives to keep an eye on

Marjorie. At the courthouse that day, Marjorie also claimed she was penniless and had applied for welfare. And accompanying her to the courthouse were Wally and Helen Hagen of Mound, and their daughter, Nancy. Within five years, Helen would be dead and Marjorie would be the new Mrs. Wally Hagen. And much later, Nancy would lead the charge of voices who claimed Marjorie had killed both of her parents.

Inside Stories:
Roger's Trial

By spring of the next year, the two sides were ready. The case of the State of Minnesota vs. Roger Sipe Caldwell was ready to roll. A judge in Duluth moved the trial to Brainerd, citing too much pre-trial publicity in Duluth, even though almost everyone in the state was pretty much aware of the situation.

I drove to Brainerd the first day of the trial in April 1978, and checked into the Holiday Inn. The first few days were full of legal motions and maneuvers, as they prepared to find 12 people who hadn't already made up their minds about the case to be the jury.

There wasn't much excitement at first. Each night, reporters covering the case gathered at a local restaurant for dinner, discussing the slow moving events and wondering how long we'd be away from home. One night, a few of us had a brainstorm. Rather than spend the summer living in a hotel room, why not see if one of the local resorts on world-famous Gull Lake could put up a group of reporters at a reasonable price?

We called around and hit the jackpot at Grand View Lodge. Just 10 minutes north of town, Grand View was one of the premier Brainerd resorts and manager Fred Boos told us he'd just purchased a three-bedroom house on the edge of the grounds that wasn't yet in use. So the three of us – reporters from the Minneapolis Star, the Duluth paper and me – could share it for far less than we were paying at the hotel.

So each morning we packed up our notebooks and tape recorders, drove to the courthouse and spent the day listening to testimony. We'd talk to the lawyers for a few minutes afterwards, then write stories for our newspapers. Then it was back to the lodge, for relaxing evenings on the veranda. It was a fun summer.

In court, a stream of police officers, Congdon family members and witnesses from Colorado took the stand. Most of the information we already knew, but there were many fine moments, like when a police officer used a cardboard cutout to reenact how Roger reached through the broken basement window to break into the mansion.

We speculated for weeks about whether Roger would testify on his own behalf. He didn't. Doug Thomson didn't want to take the risk that Roger would say something incriminating or stupid. Thomson sincerely believed that there was a chance that the jury would have reasonable doubt in the case, because there was very little physical evidence and no eyewitnesses. And back in those days there were no reliable tests for DNA. Dueling experts testified that fingerprints, hair and blood found in the mansion could have, or could not have, come from Caldwell.

In addition to reporters from around the state, a cadre of regular trial watchers showed up each day at the historic courthouse. Most were drawn by the sensational aspect of the murders, but soon found the day-by-day testimony repetitious.

"Sometimes it gets a little boring," said Mrs. E. M. Goldsberry of rural Brainerd, who skipped jury selection but saw all but one day of testimony. "Like Tuesday. I almost fell asleep and so did the jury."

On some of the pleasant summer days, reporters and spectators sat on the courthouse lawn during the lunch break, relaxing, eating and comparing notes. Several times a WCCO-TV reporter brought his tuba along and serenaded the group with rounds of deep oom-pah-pahs.

But the atmosphere turned serious July 1, when testimony ended after eight weeks and 108 witnesses. Now it was the jury's turn. For three days they wrangled with questions of evidence and experts and common sense. At least two jurors were bothered that Roger didn't testify on his own behalf. They all compared notes and argued back and forth. On their first vote, a majority wanted acquittal, so Thomson was on the right track in his feelings about reasonable doubt. But a forceful foreman kept raising the evidence issues and after three days the vote was unanimous. Guilty. As the verdict was read, Roger looked at the jurors and said quietly: "You're wrong."

Before rushing off to write out the story, I asked Prosecutor DeSanto: "What's next?" "This was just the end of Step One," he said. Does Step Two involve Marjorie? "Probably, but that's all I can say right now."

There was one additional mystery during the trial. The first juror chosen back in mid-April was Fern Swartout, a 54-year-old housewife from rural Brainerd. But four weeks later, just as the main trial was about to begin, the judge removed Swartout and another juror was added. The judge and lawyers refused to discuss her removal until after the verdict. The media crew, a little giddy after such a long encounter with justice, made t-shirts to celebrate the end of the trial. On the back of the shirts was the question: "Whatever happened to Fern Swartout?"

Finally, when Roger was sentenced to two consecutive life terms in prison two days later, the Fern question was answered. Before testimony began, Swartout had received a letter offering her $10,000 to convict Roger Caldwell. She immediately contacted the judge, who removed her from the case. Police investigated the letter and one of their theories, never proven, was that Marjorie Caldwell might have sent it.

One day later, Marjorie Caldwell was charged with conspiracy to kill her mother. She turned herself in and was released on $100,000 bond. Step Two had begun.

≈

Inside Stories:
Marjorie's Trial

Marjorie's trial was closer to the Twin Cities – just south of St. Paul in Hastings – so the reporters didn't have to stay at a hotel or resort. Too bad. It began a year later, in April 1979. The list of potential witnesses included names of those who'd testified in the first trial, police officers, Congdon family members and staff, and people from Colorado who'd seen Roger or Marjorie the week of the murders. But there was one name that didn't ring a bell: William Furman of Colorado.

Using directory assistance, I tracked down Mr. Furman on his mobile phone in Denver. He said he was a private detective who'd been hired by Thomas Congdon of Englewood, Colo., a nephew of Miss Congdon. And he said one of his men followed Roger and Marjorie from Denver to Duluth, where they attended Miss Congdon's funeral. He said that his employee couldn't find a hotel room in Duluth that first night, so Furman, himself, flew to Duluth to take over surveillance. Furman said he flew back the next morning, leaving his assistant in charge. When the Caldwells left Duluth and moved into a Bloomington hotel room, Furman's detective became sick, so Furman said he hired a Twin Cities detective agency, Triple A, to take over the case. But afterwards, when he tried to obtain records of that surveillance, Furman said he was unable to find any trace of Triple A. This was a very convoluted story, and the newspaper editors and I decided not to publish it at that time. This was early in the trial, on May 11.

Soon after, Thomas Congdon confirmed that he had hired Furman, first to protect himself and his family in case Marjorie had begun a rampage, then to investigate the Caldwells in a free-lance operation independent of the police.

On June 27, exactly two years after the murders, attorney Ron Meshbesher dragged Furman directly into the case. In his opening argument, Meshbesher hinted to the jury that Furman or his associates might have planted evidence against the Caldwells. Meshbesher had heard the same story Furman had told me: that his team had followed the Caldwells from Colorado to Duluth to Bloomington. That meant they'd been in each place the police found evidence, such as the jewelry stolen from the mansion, the airport parking ticket, the suit bag purchased at the airport and the gold coin.

After Meshbesher's courtroom revelations, I called Furman again. He said he was very unhappy at the way he was being portrayed and said he didn't frame the Caldwells. He said Duluth police were with him in Colorado when the gold coin was found at the Caldwells' hotel. And he said his men never tampered with evidence.

"I don't plan to be drug through the wringer and have my reputation ruined just because some attorney's trying to get his client off the hook," he said. Some further digging showed that Furman had been involved in some other high profile cases. When he'd been hired that previous year to follow, then try to kill the wife of a wealthy businessman, he went to police. He wore a wire and recorded conversations with the husband, which led to a murder indictment. He also worked with detectives in a 1975 murder case that led to the conviction of two former New York police officers.

Asked about the Furman connection, DeSanto wouldn't comment, but other sources said the prosecution was reluctant to use any information that the detective had come up with because his reports contained many inconsistencies that would be exploited at trial. Furman's response: "I had four cases going at once back then and I got some of my agents' names mixed up."

And there was this word from the Congdon estate: Furman had been fired from the case because they thought he was incompetent.

Furman finally showed up in Minnesota to testify on July 10. To everyone's surprise he refused to answer 59 questions about his role, claiming his Fifth Amendment right against self-incrimination.

Furman did testify that he'd made only one trip to Minnesota during the case, but that it was to Bloomington, not Duluth as he'd told me earlier. He'd told the same set of stories to DeSanto, too, because the prosecutor asked Furman, under oath, about the $15,000 he received from Thomas Congdon in fees and expenses.

"In fact, you've defrauded Thomas Congdon of that money, haven't you?" DeSanto asked.

"I'll take the Fifth," Furman said.

DeSanto also asked if Furman or any of his men had planted evidence in the case. "No," Furman said.

Then, to clear up any doubts that Meshbesher might try to plant in the jurors' minds, DeSanto asked Furman: "Did you murder Elisabeth Congdon and Velma Pietila?"

"No," Furman said.

I wrote a story about Furman's testimony for the next day's newspaper and included the context from our previous discussions. Because the jury had been instructed to avoid newspapers and television during the trial, they were unaware of the many different versions of the truth that he'd told me. But not for long. The next morning,

Meshbesher called me at home and asked me to testify about the earlier interviews. The newspaper policy allowed me to testify only if subpoenaed, but Meshbesher said he could arrange for that. When I got to work, the subpoena was waiting.

Minnesota law protects reporters from divulging their notes, so Meshbesher agreed to ask me only about the published report. So, after being sworn in, I explained how I'd first contacted Furman. Then Meshbesher read parts of the story aloud and asked if I had written them. I answered yes.

Under cross-examination, DeSanto, whom I had come to know and like over the years, demanded that I turn over my notes on the Furman interviews, apparently so he could see if there was any other pertinent information he could use. But the newspaper's lawyer, who was sitting in the front row, objected and after some discussions in the judge's chambers, the matter was dropped.

In an apparent bid to attack my credibility, DeSanto also asked me if I intended to write a book about the case. At the time, I truthfully answered: no. But the idea had been planted.

In the end, Furman's role in the case was not crucial. But it provided a big distraction during the trial and probably raised some questions about the overall credibility of the police investigation. And in his final arguments, Meshbesher did raise the specter of a "Colorado Connection" that had mysteriously framed the Caldwells.

It worked. The jury acquitted Marjorie, then invited her to a post-trial party. (She was going to attend, but the press discovered the time and place so she backed out.)

Observers agreed that new information in Marjorie's trial – an eyewitness who claimed to have seen Roger in Colorado hours before the murders, and a fingerprint expert who disputed the fingerprint on the envelope containing the gold coin mailed to Roger – made the difference.

Immediately following the verdict, I drove to Stillwater Prison to interview Roger. He said he wasn't surprised, and figured this would help with his appeal. "I'm extremely happy, ecstatic, elated," Caldwell said. "Likewise, I'm bitter because I'm still in prison."

He also said that Marjorie hadn't visited him at all since his conviction. It was another concrete clue that all was not well in the Caldwell marriage.

Buoyed by Meshbesher's success, Doug Thomson continued to press Roger's appeal, but it was a slow process. Because Roger had no money and couldn't afford to pay $5,400 for the transcript of his trial, Thomson had to borrow Meshbesher's copy.

I called some of the jurors from Roger's trial and asked if, based on the new evidence, they'd changed their minds about Roger's guilt. Three of them said he deserved a new trial. "Now I feel he's been framed. But I could be wrong," said one.

～

Inside Stories: Roger's Release

S ince many of those close to the case figured Roger was guilty, there was much amazement three years later when the Minnesota Supreme overturned his conviction and ordered a new trial. The justices cited the new evidence that emerged in his case. Prosecutors vowed to try again, but figured it would take six to eight months to prepare the case. In the meantime, they agreed to release Roger from prison until the new trial began. He immediately returned to his boyhood home of Latrobe, Pennsylvania, where his family still lived.

Not long after his release, my late aunt, Beverly Kranstover, who belonged to the same church as Marjorie, mentioned that Marjorie was telling people that she was newly married, and had brought her new husband, Wally, to church. How could this be? There had been no word of a divorce from Roger. Some phone calls revealed that Marjorie and Wally had, indeed, been issued a marriage license in Valley City, North Dakota, in August 1981, while Roger was still in prison, and were now officially known as Mr. and Mrs. Wallace Hagen. This was the same Wally Hagen of Mound, who with his wife, Helen, were among the very few friends who stood by Marjorie after the murder. Helen had since died (under circumstances that would later be investigated) and Marjorie now was married to her long-time friend, Wally, who was 72. She was 49.

Yet, wasn't Marjorie still married to Roger?

There was only one way to find out. I called Roger's parents in Latrobe and reached a man who sounded to me like Roger. I'd heard his voice often at the trial and talked with him at length in prison after Marjorie's trial, so I was quite sure. I identified myself and asked for Roger.

"Roger's not here," he said. "This is, ah, Roger's brother."

I explained the situation and asked if Roger knew anything about a divorce and remarriage. There was a long pause, then the voice, which I was sure belonged to Roger, said: "Roger doesn't know anything about that."

I wrote a story about Marjorie's new marriage, with the response from Roger (or his brother). Officials in North Dakota soon filed bigamy charges against her. A state's attorney there said the charge was punishable by a maximum of five years in prison but that there were no plans to ask Minnesota authorities to turn her over.

Marjorie kept busy in other ways. In 1982 she and Wally bought a house in Mound, a western suburb of the Twin Cities. But a year later, when a large contract for deed payment was due, they didn't have the money. So they agreed to sell the house, for a tidy $30,000 profit. But right after the Hagens moved out, and before the new owners moved in, the house was destroyed by fire. Some tenacious state investigators didn't think it was an accidental fire and a lengthy investigation led to arson charges against Marjorie.

This wasn't her first encounter with a suspicious fire. Marjorie had purchased a home in Marine-on-St. Croix in 1974 and begun extensive remodeling. Then she moved to Colorado with three of her children. One day in May 1975, Marjorie flew from Denver to Minneapolis, rented a car and, according to the rental records, drove 74 miles to the Marine house and back. That day, the house burned to the ground. It had been insured for $430,000, but when Marjorie learned that authorities were on to her, she never filed an insurance claim. Back then, it wasn't a crime to burn down your own house, as long as you didn't defraud the insurance company, so charges were never filed. Legislators changed the law soon after.

She must have been appalled when one of the investigators from the Marine case, Ray DePrima of the Minnesota Bureau of Criminal Apprehension, began working on the Mound fire. And this case went to trial. This jury found her guilty and after a one-year appeal process, she began serving her sentence. During the nearly two-year incarceration at the Shakopee Women's Prison, Wally lived nearby in an Airstream trailer. When she was released, they moved to Arizona.

Inside Stories: Roger's Deal

I was caught completely by surprise in July 1983 when word leaked out that Roger Caldwell had quietly returned to Duluth and negotiated a plea bargain. He pleaded guilty to second degree murder (instead of the first-degree murder charges handed down by the Brainerd jury) and in return, they let him go, figuring the five years he'd already served in prison were enough. Portions of his confession – which includes many memory lapses – are included in another section of this book.

Right away, I urged my newspaper editors to send me to Latrobe, to find Roger and ask him about the murders, the deal and, of course, about Marjorie. The editors said no. The next day, though, I heard again from Roger's sister-in-law in Latrobe. She'd been helpful over the years, serving as a go-between with Roger's family whenever I needed an interview or background information. This time, she had some sobering news: a reporter from the St. Paul Pioneer Press, our main competitor, was already in Pennsylvania trying to write a story about Roger.

That was enough to stir the newspaper's competitive urge. I hopped on a plane the next day, rented a car in Pittsburgh and drove 45 miles through western Pennsylvania, into the Laurel Highlands and into Latrobe. I arrived in the early evening and soon found the rooming house where Roger lived. When he didn't answer the door, I parked just down the block and waited, hoping to see him come home and jump out in time to ask a few questions. But hours went by and still no Roger, although I may have dozed off.

I gave up in the early morning hours and returned to the hotel. The next day I tried again, with no success, then concentrated on talking to family members and checking out the town, figuring there would be an interesting story in how Roger was fitting back into the community. I had lunch the next day, right before my return flight, with Roger's brother, Howard. We had a nice talk during the lunch and near the end, I asked if he might arrange for me to speak with his parents, who were quite old and living in a nearby high-rise. I assured him that I wouldn't badger the folks, but instead wanted to know more about Roger's childhood and how they felt about his problems in Minnesota. He agreed to ask and while I lingered over dessert, Howard went to the lobby to phone his parents with the request.

A few moments later, Howard walked back towards the table, his face ashen and his shoulders hunched. For a brief second, I wondered if he'd just been told that

Roger had killed someone else. Indeed, there was bad news, but that wasn't it. Howard explained: Throughout Roger's ordeals in Minnesota, there had been no actual news coverage of the murders or his conviction in Latrobe. His family and friends knew, of course, but because of the lack of news, the elder Caldwells had never had to explain the situation to casual friends or acquaintances. Until now.

Howard said that his parents had just received their afternoon edition of the daily Latrobe newspaper, which had this screaming headline across the top: "Ex-Latrobe man free in bizarre case."

The family was devastated, he said. It was a cruel, crushing blow that was, in Howard's mind, totally unnecessary. And to top it off, the third paragraph of the story said all the information about Roger and the case had been provided by the Pioneer Press reporter who'd come to town a day ahead of me. He apparently didn't know where Roger lived, so he'd gone to the local newspaper office to search through delivery records. Naturally, they'd asked why he cared and he'd told them the entire Congdon Mansion murder saga. And now the entire county knew the story.

I didn't know what to say, but after a short pause I made a suggestion. If Roger and the family wanted to get back at the St. Paul reporter, maybe Roger could grant me an exclusive interview. The other reporter's editors wouldn't be very happy about that, I said.

Howard thought for a moment, then nodded his head. "It's worth a try," he said. I went back to my hotel room, canceled my flight home, and waited for the phone to ring. It didn't take long.

"This is Roger," said the voice on the line. "I understand you want to talk."

"Yes, sir. I do."

"There's a parking lot downtown, not far from where you are, behind the old train station. I'll meet you there in 20 minutes." Click.

I drove to the appointed spot, which was in a remote part of town with virtually no traffic at that time of day. I parked so I could see anyone approaching from the main part of town, but kept an eye on the mirrors to monitor the rear. Within minutes, there he was, opening the passenger door. As he climbed in, I wondered if this was a good idea; sitting alone with a man who had confessed, just days earlier, to killing two women. But the moment passed. He looked old and frail enough that I figured I could defend myself, if it came to that.

Roger introduced himself, then said that he'd been following my career in the newspaper over the years. He proved it by mentioning several stories I'd written in the recent past, noting that "there wasn't much to do in prison, other than reading the paper."

I had all kinds of questions for him about the plea bargain and Marjorie and the mansion and his future, but before I could start, he said he wanted to drive around a bit, to show me the sights. There'd be plenty of time for questions, he said.

So I started the car and we embarked on a tour of Latrobe. He was particularly proud of some of the old forts in the area, but we also drove past the golf course where Arnold Palmer learned his game, past the house where children's television host Mr. Rogers grew up and down near the Rolling Rock Brewery. We stopped at a cemetery to see two of his family graves. And he showed me saw some of the closed-down steel mills that illustrated the economic problems the area faced.

We also stopped at two taverns, where he was friendly with the regulars and the bartenders. But once he noticed an old friend on the street, someone he hadn't seen in years, and was relieved that the friend didn't recognize him. "I don't want to meet anyone I know right now," Roger said.

He was 49-years-old, 5' 10" and weighed about 180 pounds, up 30 pounds from his prison weight. He hair had turned silver and he was very soft spoken. There was no hint of killer in his outward appearance.

He, too, decried the local newspaper story, saying his mother had collapsed after reading it. "That was the nastiest thing they could have done," he said.

He was reluctant to talk about specifics of the case, saying that if he said anything that didn't jibe exactly with his sworn testimony in the plea bargain, that the Duluth prosecutors would nail him for perjury. But of the legal maneuvering that set him free in return for the confession he did say: "Nobody was happy about it. The idea was to wrap up the case. It's wrapped up."

As to the possibility that he was paid to take the fall, he said: "There's no way I can make you believe anything, but I did not get one farthing, one promise or even the suggestion of a promise for saying that I did it (committed the murders)."

He was effusive about Latrobe, citing its small-town charm and its wonderful people. He said his mother's high school class had just held its 59th- year reunion, doing it a year early because one of her classmates had cancer and wasn't expected to live another year for the 60th.

He said friends and relatives would never believe he was capable of murder. And although he'd had lots of trouble with alcohol, he said his binge drinking days were over. He wouldn't say anything negative about Marjorie, even though she had by now remarried and he still had heard nothing about a divorce. "Marjorie is a unique person. I can't be unfair to her, even though she's been unfair to me."

Before leaving for the airport, I dropped him on a street corner so he could walk to the friend's house where he was living. He said he planned to stay in Latrobe and was using his time to become reacquainted with his boyhood haunts.

"Like Robert Frost said: 'Home is the place where they have to take you in.' I came home."

～

Inside Stories:
Marjorie's Out

I next talked to Roger three years later, when Marjorie was released from prison on the arson and fraud convictions after serving 21 months in the Shakopee State Prison.

As Marjorie and Wally packed up their trailer and headed toward Arizona, I wondered how Roger was doing. Not so well, he said by telephone.

"Things aren't good for me," said. "Welfare and food stamps. It's no great life, but it keeps me warm and fed."

Like the rest of us, Roger said he was keeping track of Marjorie's escapades with amazement. He said he knew of her conviction and of an out-of-court settlement with her children in the inheritance dispute. Although she was granted about $8 million in the settlement, much of it went to pay attorneys' fees and most of the rest was tied up in a trust that gave her about $40,000 a year to live on.

Again, he said he was not divorced from Marjorie. In fact, the Pennsylvania welfare department had even gotten involved in the affair. Because Roger was receiving $186 per month in state aid, Pennsylvania officials had asked Minnesota courts to schedule a hearing to determine whether Marjorie had to pay support to Roger following her release from prison. "We are requesting this be heard before (Hagen) is released from Shakopee Prison since she will flee and we won't be able to locate her," said the request from Pennsylvania.

But officials in Scott County, where Shakopee Prison is located, replied that under Minnesota law Marjorie could not be forced to support Roger because it appeared they were still legally married and there were no children from the marriage.

Roger said he had worked briefly as a bartender before going onto the welfare rolls. Sources in Latrobe told me Roger lost that job because of his checkered past, although it's likely that his drinking problems also played a role.

Three years earlier he had held out hope that, due to loyalty or love, Marjorie might someday help him out of his financial rut. But she never had, he said. And he said he'd now given up hope that it would ever happen.

Inside Stories:
Ten Years Later

I n the spring of 1987 I started researching a story for the 10th anniversary of the murders. The early editions of this book had become regional bestsellers and the interest in the case never seemed to wane, thanks in large part to Marjorie's ongoing antics. But just reciting the facts again didn't seem enough. I decided to update the newspaper's readers with the current whereabouts of all the main players.

Roger was my first target. I knew he still lived in Latrobe and figured another visit was warranted. I had called ahead to tell him I was coming, but wasn't specific about day or time, and I got off the commuter plane in Latrobe late one afternoon. It had been a rocky flight from Pittsburgh and my head was spinning so much that I didn't recognize the rotund man who called my name in the airport lobby. It was Roger, looking far different from my last visit four years before. He weighed at least 250 pounds and his hair was falling out. I apologized for not recognizing him, blaming it on the turbulent flight and a crying 3-year-old across the aisle. When I went to rent a car, Roger said: "Never mind; you can use my car." He also offered to let me sleep in his apartment. I accepted the car offer, but not the room.

In the parking lot, he gestured for me to drive the 14-year-old Gran Torino station wagon that belonged to his parents. As I started it up, he cautioned me to be careful on hills, because the brakes weren't too good. We drove around town again, seeing the sights. This time, without an immediate deadline, I hoped to draw him out more, to learn more about his past, what he thought about the murder case and what made him tick. He didn't disappoint.

"One of the things that always aggravated me about being convicted of murder is that everyone who ever knew me knows I couldn't kill anyone," he said. "I wrecked a car once in order to avoid hitting a dog. I never shot a rabbit; I don't even have a gun. And there's no evidence that I ever left Colorado that day. And maybe I'm not too bright, but if you're going to commit murder, you're going to have a plan. What kind of premeditated murder can you have with a candlestick holder? I never did believe that murder was the motive. It was fishy. I think something went haywire and then the nurse was killed. It just didn't make any sense to kill someone that way."

He spoke as if it he hadn't been in the mansion that night, but whether he was telling the truth, or had convinced himself of his innocence after the fact, I couldn't tell. He said his confession was based on facts he picked up at the trial. "Remember, I sat through that thing with a front row seat," he said.

Roger said his childhood in Latrobe was happy. "I was raised in a time of Cinderella, happily-ever-after time. We'd just come off the war and in America we were proud, there was nothing we couldn't do. I expected my life to be happy, that everything would be wonderful. Except that isn't the way life is.

"I ran off and got married. I was 19, she was 18. The marriage quickly fell apart. I started drinking in the third or fourth year. I was disillusioned and disappointed."

His marriage to Martha Caldwell actually lasted 20 years and produced three children. Despite the problems, Roger said he savored some parts of family life.

"I saved the baby teeth from all three kids in a small cedar chest. The oldest girl wrote a note and drew a cutesy picture to the Tooth Fairy. I kept that, too, and the girls' pig tails. I kept all kinds of things of no value, my high school diploma, medals from sports, old photos. I'm sure after the divorce someone threw it all out; there was nothing I could do about it."

He knew he'd made many mistakes with his first family. "When I found out my son was gay, I got drunk, like I always did when there was a crisis. I'm not proud of it, but there's no point in lying about it now."

"I'm really a likeable drunk. I was drunk all my life. I lost a marriage and several jobs, but I'm still drinking – as long as you're buying," he said with a wink.

Roger also had lots to say about Marjorie. They met in January 1976, two years after his divorce. She was also divorced and they met at a Parents Without Partners meeting. Two months later they married.

"She was bonkers, lots of fun," he said. "She likes living in the fast lane, life on the edge. But the roof kept falling in, further and further. More and more debt. She really isn't dishonest. She's nuts, but she fully intends to pay off her bills. She used to say when her Mama dies she'll be able to pay everyone back. But the reality is, now matter how much money she had, she'd spend it. And thickheaded and naïve as I was, I never took action. It was clear she was lying because I could never pin her down. She's an intelligent woman, a great talker. She'd be a hell of an actress if she wasn't so dumpy."

Roger knew he'd made a fool of himself, but still didn't grasp the extent of her betrayal. She had, after all, already remarried without bothering him with the details of a divorce. "I was a fool, and I'm sure I looked like a gigolo, which I was, in a way. But that's not accurate, either. A gigolo at least gets something for his gigoloing."

He said, though, that he didn't hate her. "I have no feelings for her whatever, one way or the other. I blamed her for this mess only as far as she deserted me. I can't really blame her for her mother and the nurse being killed. After all, 12 jurors in Brainerd said: Hey, ho, off he goes. The only thing that really offends me is that she totally abandoned me. It just isn't right. You don't treat people that way."

He said they faced financial problems from the very start, when Marjorie bounced a check at their wedding reception. He paused a minute for another wedding memory: "The trustees in Duluth sent us a set of towels for the wedding. Marj went through the roof."

As the debts mounted, Roger panicked. "I was rowing as fast as I could, but we kept getting in deeper and deeper. I told her we were both going to end up in jail. I knew what we were doing was wrong. I was just a poor slob running around like a maniac, trying to pacify people who were threatening to sue. I was in a state of panic by the time of the murders. We were in hock tens of thousands of dollars and there was no indication that she was going to give up writing bad checks. It finally dawned on me that she was not about to change. No amount of preaching or hollering was going to make her change."

Back at his apartment, where he lived with a girlfriend, Evelyn, and a orange tabby cat, Roger limped up the stairs. He said his knees were wracked with arthritis. His place was small, with shelves of knick-knacks. A magnifying glass sat atop the TV Guide on his coffee table. He showed me a row of shirts in his closet, saying he'd bought them for a quarter apiece at the St. Vincent de Paul thrift shop.

He had dozens of plants in a little garden behind the apartment and took pride in showing them off.

It was a depressing visit, but I learned volumes about Roger. I had $20 in cash left as I prepared to head home. I gave him the money. As I left, he said he had one more thing to say, but it had to be off the record. I agreed.

"You can't print this or they'll put me back in prison for perjury. But I didn't do it. I was home in bed, in Colorado that night. I remember distinctly that I was reading a book, 'SS-GB' by Len Deighton. I didn't do it."

He acknowledged that there was no way he could prove that he was in Colorado. Again, it was hard to know if he was telling the truth or telling me what he'd convinced himself was the truth.

The interview with Roger was the highlight of the 10-year roundup, but there were other tidbits, as well. I learned that Wally Hagen's first wife, Helen, had died rather suddenly soon before Marjorie and Wally were married, and that Marjorie had been the last person to visit Helen in the nursing home. Wally's children were suspicious. Police investigated the case as a possible homicide, but no charges were filed.

Loren Pietila – husband of Velma Pietila, the nurse who died defending Miss Congdon that night – had sued the Congdon estate, claiming they hadn't provided adequate security. A jury agreed and awarded him $225,000, but the Minnesota Supreme Court overturned the award. By then it didn't matter. Loren Pietila had died 11 days earlier.

Some of the nurses who cared for Miss Congdon in her later years also told me that they suspected she'd given birth to a baby, based on scars they'd seen. There had been speculation over the years that one of her two adopted daughters might actually have been hers, but the records had been sealed and there was never any proof. Jennifer Johnson, Miss Congdon's other daughter, said she sincerely doubted that her mother had borne a child. She said doctors had operated on her mother several times over the years, which could account for the scars.

Inside Stories:
Roger's Suicide

I never saw Roger again, but I returned to Latrobe one year later for his funeral. His dire predictions had come true, although medical problems hadn't killed him. It was suicide.

The Monday before he died, Roger's sister-in-law, Betty, called to say Roger was acting strangely. He'd told his family that he was terminally ill, so Roger's brother planned to meet with the doctor that week to check the prognosis. After a Twins game Wednesday night, about 10 p.m., I called Betty in Latrobe to see how the doctor visit had gone.

Betty was quite disturbed when she answered. "Haven't you heard? I thought you knew," she said.

"What, Betty? What is it?"

"Roger. He's dead."

After telling his family that he was dying and had only two months to live, Roger made the decision to end his life. He was 53. His apartment was only eight blocks from his parents' place, so he walked over there one last time. His 82-year-old father wasn't there. He was in a nursing home recovering from a broken hip. Roger told his mother nothing about his plans, but overstayed his welcome. His family had grown increasingly tired of his complaints and depression in the previous months, and about midnight his mother called his brother to take Roger home.

Howard and Betty arrived and led him out. Roger kissed his mother as he left and said goodbye. It was the last time she would see him alive. Howard and Betty bought him some cigarettes and beer and took him home. He was very talkative and as they left, he also kissed Betty goodbye.

The next day, Roger called Betty. "He was looking for someone to talk to. That's all he wanted, and maybe some beer or whiskey or cigarettes. He felt abandoned," she said. He talked mostly about his childhood and Marjorie. "He said nothing about the murders, but I really believe that's what he wanted to talk about."

Betty said Roger and Evelyn had recently moved into a new apartment, but late Tuesday night Roger returned to the old apartment and slit his wrists. His body was found at 11 a.m. Wednesday.

Although I learned of the suicide late at night, I was able to reach the two main attorneys in the case. John DeSanto, the prosecutor, said it was unfortunate that

Roger died without telling all he knew. "From my perspective, I always believed Marjorie was involved, and I always thought that he'd implicate her at some time," he said. "The whole thing's kind of sad. It was really a wasted life."

Roger's attorney, Doug Thomson, said, "I really don't know whether he did it or not. There's always been some doubt, and that's all you need in a criminal case. Even when he entered his plea in the plea bargain, that statement was loaded with inconsistencies. It created more doubt about what happened."

Using the interviews with Betty, DeSanto and Thomson, I was able to write a front page story for the next day's paper. "Congdon murder figure Roger Caldwell, 53, dies" was the headline. But after finishing the story, I wondered why Betty Caldwell had assumed that I already knew about Roger's death, when I first reached her. The answer came the next day, when the Pioneer Press newspaper ran a front-page story about Roger, which they overzealously labeled as exclusive. Apparently someone from Latrobe had called them about Roger's suicide and the reporters talked with the family and lawyers before I did, leading them to believe our paper wasn't aware of the development. In her grief, Betty thought she was talking with someone from our newspaper, which is why she figured I already knew.

Three days later, Roger was buried after a small private service attended by eight family members and me. There were Bible readings and some tears at the closed-casket service. Roger's mother and three brothers were there, but his father couldn't leave the nursing home. Roger's two daughters from his first marriage weren't there, either. He'd had no contact with them since the 1974 divorce and they might not have even known about his death

A few more details about his last days emerged. Just days before he killed himself, Roger told his brother that he'd been on a three-week drinking binge and had lost 80 pounds. The minister who presided over the service said he'd seen Roger only once before, when a congregation member helped an obviously drunk Roger walk across the parking lot. The last person to see him alive was a patron at the bar next to Roger's apartment, a stranger who told police Roger had called to him out the window, and asked what day it was. Police said Roger had cut his wrists with a steak knife and died in the living room, with an empty beer bottle nearby.

Evelyn, who'd been Roger's girlfriend for more than four years, wasn't at the service but I found her in town. She said she'd broken her arm on Sunday and was in no shape to attend the funeral. "Maybe it was the booze that made him do it. Maybe the thoughts of all he'd been through. He was always sitting around with nothing to do, and it preyed on his mind," she said. He didn't discuss the murders with her, except to say occasionally that he didn't do it. And he rarely talked to her about Marjorie. When he was sober, he was a good man, she said. "He was a very good person. He gave up on life, but he was still a good person."

Roger's suicide note said: "What you need to know is that I didn't kill those girls, or to my knowledge, ever harm a soul in my life."

Over the years, many people have asked whether I think Roger committed the Congdon murders. I think he did. Despite his denials, there is too much evidence pointing to his guilt to think otherwise. And after his suicide, I decided that if Roger was capable of committing such violence on himself, he was capable of doing it to others, particularly if he was drunk.

And shortly before he killed himself, Roger offered to sell additional information about the murders to Charles Johnson, the well-to-do husband of Marjorie's sister, Jennifer. Using an attorney as an intermediary, Roger claimed he wanted to set the record straight and would reveal information about another person involved in the murder -- for a price.

Johnson balked at the idea of paying Roger up front, though, and instead suggested that a reward might be paid if another person was charged in the case. However, the negotiations bogged down, and then Roger committed suicide, so there's no way to know if his offer was legitimate, or, if in his impoverished state, he was simply trying to extort money from the family.

So even though Roger hinted that he had been framed, it doesn't seem likely. To accept the frame-up theory means believing that some nefarious group pulled off a wide-spread, perfectly executed conspiracy. Knowing many of those involved, such a theory seems implausible.

~

Inside Stories:
Arizona Ashes

Less than a year after Roger's death, Marjorie was again in the news when Arizona officials investigated a $55,000 bad check she'd allegedly written for mobile home repairs. Then came the rash of fires in Ajo, Az., and finally Marjorie's arrest and trial in the arson case.

I kept track of the case by phone, checking with investigators and lawyers as necessary and writing occasional stories. On Oct. 29, 1992, the jury found her guilty of attempted arson, for trying to burn down her neighbor's home. The judge allowed her to return home for a day before beginning her prison term, to arrange for care for her ailing husband, Wally.

Our newsroom is usually deserted on Saturdays, but on Saturday, Oct. 31, one of my bosses stopped in the office and checked the answering machine. She reached me at home and gave me a message to call Lt. Tom Taylor of the Pima County Sheriff's office. I did and his report was unbelievable: Marjorie was in jail charged with murdering her husband. I hurried to the office and got to work.

During Marjorie's short furlough at home, police noticed the smell of natural gas outside her home. When they checked, Marjorie said she'd left the oven on, but everyone was okay. A few hours later Taylor got a call from one of Wally Hagen's son, saying Marjorie had just called him to say Wally was dead. She was arrested and charged with murder. That night, I attended a Bruce Springsteen concert in Minneapolis, but missed much of the first set because I had to make final changes in the story with the copy desk. I'm a huge Springsteen fan, but the story was the top priority.

Over the next several months I was in constant touch with Wally's children from his first marriage, who were convinced that Marjorie was responsible for their father's death. They also felt Marjorie had killed their mother years before, even though no evidence had ever turned up in that case. The long-simmering feud between Marjorie and her stepchildren erupted into a full-scale, public war.

The signature battle was fought over Wally's body. His children wanted him shipped to Minnesota, to be buried next to their mother. But Marjorie wanted him buried in Arizona. For seven months, the body was kept frozen in a morgue, as potential evidence in the murder case. Eventually, the murder charges were dropped when tests showed that Wally apparently committed suicide with an overdose of a prescription drug. The body was cremated. The Hagen children were stuck with a $750 bill; Marjorie paid $250.

The legal skirmish for custody of the ashes continued for more than three years. The Hagens tried to prove that Marjorie and Wally were never legally married, because there was apparently no divorce from Roger. But in a deposition, Marjorie claimed she had filed for divorce, somewhere in Mexico, though she couldn't remember the details. At one point, neither side trusted the other to take the urn to the courthouse for safekeeping, so attorneys from each camp were told to make the delivery together. A Tucson judge tried to settle the matter by suggesting that they split the ashes, but both sides balked at that idea.

Finally, at the end of 1995, the Hagens' money and patience ran out. They agreed to the Solomon-like decision and shared the ashes. The lawyers agreed to the settlement on Dec. 19, but the mortician, fearing that the package might get lost in the Christmas mail rush, waited until after the holiday to send their half to Minnesota. The family held a memorial service and buried the remains next to his first wife's plot in a Mound cemetery, more than three years after his death.

For several years, the case was quiet. Marjorie was serving her time in the Arizona State Prison system, working as a typist and clerk in school programs, the chaplain's office and the law library.

Then one day in August 1999 I got a call from a reporter in Denver. She was working on a story that I'd covered in the past and wanted some background information. It was the Caldwell murder case, she said. I filled her in, then listened to her fascinating, but morbid, account: A woman from the Denver area had killed her mother, then preserved the body for two weeks in 700 pounds of rock salt, in a makeshift cardboard coffin in her basement. After police found the body, the daughter killed herself.

The amazing part of the story, from a Minnesota point of view, was that the dead mother was Martha Burns, Roger Caldwell's first wife. And the murder suspect was Chris O'Neil, the 44-year-old daughter of Martha Burns and Roger Caldwell. They lived together in the same house in Arapahoe County where they had lived with Roger before the divorce. (In 1977, I'd stopped at the house while working on the story in the Denver area, but Burns had asked me to leave, saying she had no comment.)

The parallels were spooky. O'Neil had smothered her mother with a pillow, the same way Roger had killed Miss Congdon. And then, overcome by despair and other demons, O'Neil had committed suicide, just like her father.

Roger had talked only briefly about his two daughters, saying that one of them blamed him for the suicide of her brother, Roger's only son. But Roger had never said which daughter bore him such hatred. The other daughter lives in California.

~

Inside Stories:
Chance for Parole

In the fall of 2001, preparations began for Marjorie's first parole hearing at the Arizona Women's Prison in Parryville, on the outer western edge of Phoenix's suburbs. Her 15-year sentence actually ran until 2007, but it was assumed that she'd be released after about 10 years. It had now been nine. Prison officials sent notices to many of Marjorie's family members, as well as to witnesses in her trial, so they could comment about her possible early release.

Comment they did. Ten people sent letters opposing her release, including one of Marjorie's daughters and Marjorie's sister, Jennifer Johnson. The man who lived in the house that was nearly burned down also wrote, saying he'd moved to another state but that "it would not be hard for her to find me."

Most vehement, though, were Tom Hagen and Nancy Kaufmann, two of Wally's children. They decided to attend the hearing for two reasons, to tell the board that she would continue to be a risk if she were released, and to let Marjorie know they were watching her. The parole board received only one letter in favor of parole. It came from Ed Bolding, Marjorie's Arizona lawyer and long-time friend.

I arrived in Phoenix a day before the hearing and checked her files at the state offices. That night, Tom and Nancy called my hotel room; they'd just arrived and wondered if I wanted to have dinner. I'd already eaten, but went with them to have dessert and listen to their plans for the hearing. They weren't sure what they'd say, but felt it was important to respond to whatever Marjorie might say about their father.

The next morning, the hearing was delayed for two hours, so I waited in the office of prison warden, William Gaspar. He wondered why I'd come all the way from Minnesota for a hearing on an attempted arson case. He had no idea about Marjorie's background, so I gave him the abridged version.

The warden then told me stories about his early days in the prison business, when he used to hunt escaped prisoners. Once, he and a partner found a fleeing inmate riding a bicycle down a city street. They stopped their car, knocked him off the bike, threw him into the car and put the bike in the trunk. On the way back to the prison, though, they were stopped by a local police officer responding to reports of a kidnapping.

As the hearing time approached, we waited in a sun-drenched plaza deep inside the prison walls. Marjorie waited, too, at a picnic table 20 yards away. She wore an orange jump suit and white tennis shoes, with her grey hair pulled back in a bun. She didn't speak with other inmates waiting nearby, but often consulted a file folder. I didn't approach her, because I'd been warned earlier by prison officials not to speak directly with her. Any press interviews were to be conducted by telephone, but Marjorie had already declined two interview requests that week.

When Marjorie's hearing finally began, she sat at a desk near the front of the room, directly across from the five parole board members. Tom Hagen and Nancy Kaufmann took seats just to her left. I sat behind Marjorie, near several guards and administrators. The warden attended, too.

After a quick glance at the Hagens, Marjorie launched into a rambling indictment of Wally's children, claiming they had conspired to isolate Wally from his family and refused to help with his medical care. It was an unusual approach to her parole hearing. Judging by their comments and questions, the board members clearly wanted to hear her express remorse for her crime, and to show how prison had helped her become a better person. But she continued to claim she was innocent of the attempted Ajo arson.

I saw the Hagens wince and roll their eyes at her words. When time came for public comments, Tom and Nancy felt compelled to respond. They said they'd always loved and helped their father and that it was Marjorie who tried to tear the family apart. They also warned the board about her penchant for fires.

Partway through the hearing, I walked to the front of the room to take a picture of Marjorie. She covered her face with her hands for a moment, then, apparently realizing she looked silly, she turned her attention back to the board members.

When the board finally voted, the decision was unanimous against parole. When they told her there'd be another opportunity in 2002, Marjorie turned, and showing no emotion, walked out of the room. The Hagens were visibly relieved. They left quickly to catch a flight back to Minnesota.

As I left the prison, the warden waved and said "See you next year."

Three months later, I got a call from Bolding, Marjorie's lawyer, who said he'd just learned that the pardon board had failed to make the legally-required tape recording of the November hearing. He said he'd filed an appeal and was granted a new hearing for March 12.

So the Hagens again flew to Phoenix for the repeat hearing. The outcome was the same: no parole. I didn't attend this time, but afterwards, Bolding reported: "The board was not impressed. They want you to come in on all fours and do the mea culpa routine and say 'I will go and sin no more.' They call it accepting responsibility, but in this case, whatever Marj's intentions were in her mind, there's just no evidence that she planned to start the fire."

But Marjorie was holding up well in prison, he said. "She's rolling right along. She knows she'll be released soon."

∼

Inside Stories: DNA and Finally She's Free

Just before the 25th anniversary of the murders in 2002, I called Prosecutor DeSanto to see if any DNA evidence existed from the murder scene. DNA crime scene analysis didn't exist in 1977, but it does now, and I figured the newspaper might pay to test the evidence.

Sorry, DeSanto told me. All the evidence had been destroyed.

About a year later, though, DeSanto announced that he and others had written their own book, and there *was* DNA evidence still available. It had been in a box in *his* basement all along.

Tests showed that the envelope Caldwell had sent from Duluth to Colorado contained saliva that matched Caldwell's DNA. This was no surprise to those close to the case, who always believed Caldwell was guilty. The real question, which is unanswered, and may remain so unless more evidence turns up: Was there a murderous accomplice with Caldwell that night in the Mansion?

In 2003, Marjorie skipped another scheduled parole hearing, knowing that her chances weren't good and that in early 2004 they had to let her go anyway, without a hearing, because early release rules had been eased.

Over they years I've tried many times to arrange interviews with Marjorie, figuring she might want to provide her side of the story. She always declined.

On the verge of her release, I tried again, sending a polite letter to her in prison. A couple weeks later, I got a reply of sorts. She had scrawled a message to her lawyer on the back of my letter, saying: "Will you please do something about these people?"

Her lawyer, Ed Bolding, sent her note to me, along with his own inscription.

"Joe, Marjorie is not interested. Will not talk to anyone. Sorry. Regards to you. Ed."

Prison officials kept the media away from the prison doors the morning of her release, requiring the television photographer to use a long lens to capture her walk from the door to the rented car.

Later in the day, a small fire caused some damage at a church in Ajo, the town once ravaged by the arson fires. Residents joked that she must be back.

During a radio interview that day, I was asked: If Marjorie called and invited you over to her house and offered to give you her side of the story over a pot of tea, would you go and would you drink the tea?

My reply: Absolutely I'd go, but I'd take along a photographer so I wouldn't be alone with her. And I'd pass on the tea.

In 2007, those who've followed the case probably weren't surprised to learn that Marjorie was arrested again, this time in Tucson. She was accused of fraud and forgery after befriending an elderly man and taking his money after he died.

Following this arrest, people who'd recently met Marjorie told me that she seemed polite and charming, and had adopted a greyhound named Blueberry.

Finally, after nearly two years of delays, Marjorie pleaded guilty in a plea bargain deal and despite her lengthy criminal background, was sentenced to "three years of intensive probation" and ordered to pay $10,000 for attorney's fees.

~

The Confession

These are edited excerpts of Roger Caldwell's confession to the murders of Elisabeth Congdon and Velma Pietila. The confession was made July 5, 1983, at the St. Louis County Courthouse in Duluth.

Prosecutor John DeSanto asked the questions. Roger Caldwell answered.

Q Do you understand that if you say something here that is not truthful, you could subject yourself to perjury charges for any untruthful statements made in answer to the questions here this afternoon in the library, do you understand that?

A *I do.*

Q Also, Mr. Caldwell, do you understand that it is agreed as part of this plea negotiation agreement that you would receive no further incarceration for the new convictions of murder in the second degree, that you would be sentenced simply to time served or if there was an 111 month sentence, any further sentence would be simply suspended. Do you understand that? You would receive no further time in jail?

A *I do.*

Q Now with regard to the murders of Elisabeth Congdon and Velma Pietila, would you state, in your words when the incident, which led to those murders was first planned or discussed with anyone?

A *There was no plan of murder.*

Q All right. With regard to the murders that occurred, these murders that occurred on June 27th of 1977, would you, in your own words, simply state how it came about that you committed those murders?

A *The intent was burglary. I was surprised in the act of the commission of the burglary by the nurse who was totally unknown to me. She was loud and aggressive. I tried to silence her.*

Q Mr. Caldwell, do you know that that's kind of hard to believe that you don't remember the name used to buy the airplane ticket?

A *Well, yes, I can understand how it's hard to believe, but as you well know with the investigation you conducted, I am an old drunk. I have been on the sauce for a long, long time. I have been treated for alcoholism on two different occasions and have wandered in and out of Alcoholics Anonymous heaven knows how many times over the years, and in time of stress, I mean I would maintain a glow all day, everyday, seven days a week, year after year. Not just periodically, this was a constant, ongoing thing. I am not using, trying to imply that drunkenness was a defense, that's out of the question because drunkenness was my normal state and sometimes worse.*

Q That's what you are attributing your failure to remember the name that you used to travel?

A *There were many things that I don't remember throughout my life that were nearer and dearer to me than a false name I would give at an airline counter. I don't recall the names of uncles and aunts and nieces and nephews.*

Q Okay.

A *No. As our situation progressed, as it became apparent after our marriage that Marjorie was – well, she was simply a terrible liar, that's all she did to me constantly. Not at first, but then the longer we were married the worse it got and it became – I tried to defend her. I believed her. I loved her.*

Q Now, you fly then to Minneapolis. What time do you get to Minneapolis?

A *It was daylight.*

Q Daylight. What do you do when you get to Minneapolis?

A *Well, tried to figure out where Duluth was. I didn't know. I had only been here once before in my life.*

Q Okay. What did you do now once you got to Minneapolis Airport when you have come, as you say, to burglarize the mansion?

A Well, tried to figure a way to get from there to Duluth and I must have flown up (on the one previous visit) but I wasn't all that impressed with your Duluth Airport and it dawned on me that the police would certainly be checking transportation and one of the shuttle flights from the Twin Cities up to here would be probably too easy to trace and pinpoint me, so I toyed with the idea of taking a cab but then I thought, too, I honestly didn't have any knowledge of the distance.

Q So what did you eventually do?

A I wandered around and asked people directions and wound up taking a bus.

Q A bus from where?

A From the bus station in the Twin Cities on up here to Duluth.

Q And what name did you use to get your bus ticket?

A I don't know that there is a name required.

Q And do you recall when you got to Duluth, what time of day it was?

A Late afternoon or early evening, I suppose.

Q Then what did you do?

A Well, I had a few more drinks.

Q Where did you have the drinks?...In a bar in Duluth?

A Oh, yes. Oh yeah.

Q Then what did you do?

A *I waited until dark. And in discussions at the bar found out how the cab service worked in town and took a taxi cab out to London Road. I didn't even know the address...I told him I would tell him where to let me out. I didn't know for certain where I was going but I would recognize the site when I saw it.*

Q Where did you get out?

A *Well, I recognized the mansions, other big homes sitting off to the right, and when I got to where I thought the Congdon home was, I had him then let me out a few blocks up London Road.*

Q Do you recall during the early part of the investigation, after your arrest, when we had a cab driver look at you in a lineup?

A *I do.*

Q Was that the cab driver?

A *I have no idea.*

Q Were you frightened he might identify you?

A *Yes I was. But I don't have any idea if that's who it was. It may very well have been. I don't know.*

Q You went from the bus to a bar and then you took a cab out to the mansion when it got dark?

A *Your bus terminal, as I recall, seemed to be in a rather seedy place, in a rather seedy neighborhood, which was fine for my purposes and there were several bars in the area and I just chose one of them, a real working-man's bar.*

Q Okay. You get (out of the cab.) Then what did you do?

A *It was just approaching darkness and in my mind I thought it best to wait until the house was still and people were sleeping and I had only ever been there one other time and had never poked around or seen the grounds, so I was totally unfamiliar with the geography and I didn't want to linger on the street, on London Road. I didn't know whether it was a prominent thoroughfare. As I say, I am not acquainted with Duluth.*

Q Where did you wait?

A *First, I walked back past the house so I would make sure I knew where I was and walked clear past it and there was a little cemetery on the same side of the street as the house that wasn't in good maintenance and looked like it didn't get a lot of traffic and I waited in there. (When it got dark enough) I left there and went over to the house.*

Q Are you drinking on the hooch?

A *Yeah. I was seldom without one.*

Q What kind of booze was it, do you know?

A *Vodka. A pint.*

Q Where did you get in (to the mansion)?

A *Through the window.*

Q What did you use to break the window?

A *Something on the porch, or there was an odd, it's not a room, you couldn't even call it a sun porch that this window faced out on, that was filled with clutter and I would imagine I found an object there to break the window with.*

Q What did you do after you got into the mansion through the window?

A *I remember walking past a pool table and getting to the stairs and my intention was to get up to Miss Congdon's bedroom, where I assumed, whatever valuables of small size that can be easily carried would be found.*

Q Did you know where the bedroom would be located?

A *No I didn't.*

Q Had Marjorie talked with you about that?

A *Marjorie and I never – The only talking we did about the mansion was the time she had spent there as a child and in growing-up years, but we never discussed specifics about the physical arrangements of the house other than to tell me about the boat house and the groundskeeper's house and the old greenhouses. We never went into any details about the floor plan of the house or the arrangements.*

Q Then what happens?

A *Then I started up the stairs. I wasn't expecting a confrontation…The house was dark, it was late at night. I assumed people were sleeping and I meant no harm.*

Q Had you discussed that in any way with Marjorie Caldwell? Whether someone would be there or not?

A *No.*

Q Did you know about Elisabeth Congdon having around-the-clock nurses?

A *Yes, I did know that.*

Q Now, you get to the staircase, what happened?

A Well, I started up the stairs and immediately roused the nurse, which surprised me as much as it did her, I'm sure. I guess I was on the landing (between the first and second floors) and she was either still coming down the stairs or had reached the landing.

Q What happens there?

A Well, she shouted and struck out at me. I don't know that she had anything in her hand or not. She may have had.

Q What did you do?

A Struck back. (There was) a fight.

Q Is the nurse killed at that time?

A No, no. I suppose she was unconscious because then I went up to the second floor and, as I recall, she had let out a moan or something to indicate that she was still, if not awake or alert, still making noises...I found the candlestick and went back down and beat her with it to quiet her down.

Q What did you do then after beating the nurse to death?

A Well, I didn't beat her to death. I beat her and she died.

Q What did you do after that?

A Well, that quieted her and there was light on in a room. I poked in there, looked in and saw Miss Congdon was in there and I didn't wish to – she was obviously sleeping and I knew she was not a well woman, I didn't want to disturb her...so I thought, better if I can obstruct her hearing. Anyway, I took the pillow and put it over her head, more to block out light and sound than anything else.

Q You know that the physical evidence in the investigation showed a blood type that (was) consistent with your blood on the bedspread and the pillow under Elisabeth Congdon's head. Would that have been because you were cut in the struggle with the nurse?

A The nurse bit my finger.

Q Do you recall turning the shoe of the nurse on her which resulted in those little puncture wounds on her head and arms?

A I don't recall any detail of that. I was so terrified and panicked by what I was obviously caught up in, that it was just – it all happened so quickly.

Q So you are admitting the murder of Elisabeth Congdon, is that true?

A Well, I guess I am admitting to the murder of her, except murder wasn't the intention.

Q What did you do after you put the pillow over her face? What did you do in her room?

A I wanted to get out as quick as I could. I was obviously in a heck of a mess and wanted to get out of there and out of Duluth and out of Minnesota just as quickly as I could, so I ransacked drawers to look for valuables, took what I could find and left.

Q Do you remember taking the ring off Elisabeth Congdon's finger…(or) taking the watch off her wrist?

A I have no recollection of it…I was in such a state of terror I couldn't move quick enough to get out.

Q Do you remember taking the wicker basket?

A I don't remember taking it.

Q The drawers on Elisabeth Congdon's dresser were all pulled out evenly. Why were the drawers so even?

A I don't know anything about burglary. I have never stolen anything in my life. I certainly never burglarized anybody. I have never caused any damage to anyone that I can recall in a lifetime, other than what I may have done when I was drunk. I have never burglarized a home.

Q Why did you take jewelry items?

A *Well, it seemed to be a logical thing of small size and great value.*

Q What were you going to do with the jewelry items?

A *I hadn't thought that far ahead…the purpose was to sell and convert to cash.*

Q Did you have any conversation with the nurse, Velma Pietila, before your confrontation with her?

A *No, I didn't.*

Q Did you take the coin from the mansion?

A *That's another mystery. I don't have any recollection of that coin at all.*

Q (Then) where did you go, what did you do?

A *There was another room across the hall, which also had a light on, and I was looking for a bathroom. I had blood on me. Surprisingly little, but, nonetheless, blood.*

Q The washroom where you washed up was near at hand to the room where you found the keys. Where did you find the keys?

A *They were laying on the bed…They were obviously car keys. I think I even peeked out the window and saw the car in the front of the house and I went back on* downstairs and out.

Q You passed Velma Pietila's body there?

A *I did.*

Q Then you get out the front door, what do you do?

A *Went immediately to the car, matched the keys and took off for the Twin Cities.*

Q Did you, by chance, during the time you were in the mansion, hear the dog barking?

A *I did not. I heard nothing. The only sound I heard was the sounds given off by the nurse.*

Q In going to the mansion, as you say to simply burglarize it, to steal from it, what was your original intention of how you were going to get away with this?

A *I had no plan. I was drunker than a lord without any – I had no plan. I had nothing. I was stupid. I was – I had no prior experience along those lines. I have never in my life broken into anything.*

Q If you're going to commit burglary, though, didn't you have some plan as far as how you were going to get away with the goods?

A *No, I didn't.*

Q It was just lucky that the keys for the car happened to be there.

A *Just dumb luck that the keys for the car happened to be there.*

Q What do you remember about the trip (from Duluth to Minneapolis)?

A *I remember that I had a bottle with me and I was sipping at that, too.*

Q A bottle of what? How much, what kind was it, where had you gotten the bottle?

A *I don't know if I brought it with me on the plane or bought it here in Duluth. It was a pint bottle. It fit in the hip pocket.*

Q You entered the mansion, then, with the bottle in your pocket?

A *Oh sure. I wouldn't be without it.*

Q How did you get back from Minneapolis to Colorado?

A *Flew.*

Q Commercial airlines?

A *Oh, yes. Well, again, I don't have any idea which one. It was a commercial flight.*

Q What about purchasing the suede bag?

A *It's hard to believe that. That is, I don't recall that.*

Q How did you feel when you saw we were unable to put you on an airline?

A *Dumb lucky. I know I recall our trial, the three months that you and I spent in court, vividly. I was quite sober at the time and I know through the evidence that you presented the lengths you went to put me on an airline and the hours that were spent in trying to get me there and I couldn't imagine how you missed me.*

Q (Back in Colorado) why did you make the phone call to Marj?

A *Well, I had no transportation. I don't know whether you ever uncovered this in your investigation, but it wasn't particularly uncommon for me to go off and disappear. I mean this certainly wasn't the first time that happened. At least on several occasions when Marj and I would get into horrendous arguments — her temper was far worse than mine ever will be and she would simply infuriate me and I am not, pardon me for saying so, I am not a violent man and I didn't fight with her or anybody else. I would get very upset with her and my escape has always been booze and on several occasions during our marriage I would just simply get in the car and drive off and go somewhere and get bombed and be gone sometimes, many times, overnight, sometimes two, maybe three nights.*

Q What did you do with the jewelry after you are back in Colorado? How does the jewelry get in the blue container with Marj's?

A *I put it there.*

Q When did you do that?

A *That night, I think. I know this is difficult for you and it's difficult for me, but you don't – maybe you do know, I don't know what you know, John, but I was on the sauce awful heavy.*

Q Mr. Caldwell, when you go open that safety deposit box (and put the June 24th assignment of inheritance in it) you know Elisabeth Congdon is dead, you have murdered her, right?

A *Right. I didn't know I had murdered her, no. I knew she was dead. I never thought it was murder.*

Q You are not denying doing what caused her death?

A *I am not denying that, no.*

Q With regard to Elisabeth Congdon, though, then as a result of your actions, the physical evidence somewhat contradicts what you are telling us. I mean, obviously there was more done than simply placing a pillow over her head so that she wouldn't hear, so that you could shut out the light and any noise and if it doesn't jive with the physical evidence, it leads us to question, was there somebody else in the house with you that actually killed her?

A *There was nobody else in that house with me. I don't recall doing any more (to her).*

Q The physical evidence shows us that she had – that a pillow was placed firmly enough over her that she struggled underneath it so that skin was scraped from her nose and you're aware of that physical evidence?

A *Yes, I am.*

Q Based on that, do you have any dispute that there must have been some struggle by her underneath that pillow as you held it over her?

A *I don't recall the struggle.*

Q What reaction did Marjorie have, when she picked you up at the restaurant (in Colorado)?

A *Anxious, hurried. She had been real-estating again. She had seen some properties and was telling me about them and wanting to hurry back up to the animals.*

Q What did you say to her about where you had been?

A *Virtually nothing. She never had great deal of interest. I told her something to the effect (that I had) a session with the lawyer and I had been off tooting and she didn't want to hear about it. She didn't like listening to stories of drunks.*

Q You understand that if she is involved, whether it be before the fact or after the fact, at this stage she is not going to face any criminal consequences. She has the benefit of what we call the double jeopardy clause. Do you understand that?

A *Yes, of course I do. Yes.*

Q I don't want you to sit here with some kind of motive to cover up for her, to protect her. She virtually is home free, do you understand what I am saying?

A *Yes, John. I have more reason to implicate her than I have not to implicate her.*

Q Don't you think you're getting the short end of the stick right now?

A *I know I am getting the short end of the stick, but not financially. I never had any claim to it. I didn't marry Marj for her money. When I married her, I didn't even know she had money. I had never heard of the Congdons.*

Q Why is it then, if you say Marjorie knew nothing about your going to Duluth, why does she alibi for you?

A *Trying to find reasons for what Marjorie ever had done is something that none of us are able to do, including me.*

Q Wouldn't you admit that that would point to some knowledge on her part, it's somewhat reasonable to assume she knows where you have gone...?

A No...She would come up with an awful lot of spur of the moment explanations for anything and everything to total strangers...All that I can guess is Marj knew I was off on a toot. That was a source of embarrassment to her. She didn't like to be embarrassed and she would, rather than just stay quiet, she would feel compelled to – she's a compulsive talker – she would feel compelled to explain away my absence.

Q Hadn't you planned any alibi statements on her part for you?

A No.

Q What about when you came to Duluth for the funeral? Do you do anything with Marjorie as far as covering up your activities and involvement in the murder? Do you do anything, talk with her about it?

A She had no knowledge of it and, as best I knew, nobody did at that point.

Q You told no one?

A No, I had no reason to.

Q Have you been offered any money to protect her?

A None whatever.

Q Has Marjorie ever called you and asked you about this?

A I haven't seen or spoken with Marjorie since approximately three weeks after her acquittal. She came to visit me in prison. She was rather cool toward me and, as it turned out, at the time I wasn't aware of it, but as it turned out the only reason for the visit was to ask me if I wanted to continue having Doug (Thomson) representing me, or if I wanted Ron Meshbesher to visit me. I said no, I think I will stick with Doug. And as I noodled over the years I realize that that was goodbye for us and I have never laid eyes on her or spoken with her since.

Q Did Marjorie ever ask you after you were charged whether you did it?

A No. That never came up. At the time I was arrested and charged and for the months that I spent in jail in Duluth, she visited me, she brought me items. We talked as best we could under the circumstances, through the bars and what have you. She seemed to be standing by me and supporting me in every way she could. There was never any question that I was guilty.

Q Did she ask you about where you were when it looked like what happened here was consistent with you committing the murders?

A No. She never connected one with the other. As I say, it had long since stopped being a surprise – when we would get into a real argument that I would go off and go out on a toot. So this was far from the first time that had happened. I had left her high and dry before.

Q Who do you think is getting left high and dry now?

A Me.

The Chronology

June 27, 1977:
Elisabeth Congdon, wealthy Duluth heiress, is found murdered in her bed, smothered with a pillow. Her night nurse, Velma Pietila, was bludgeoned to death on the stairway of the 39-room Congdon Mansion, known as Glensheen. Officially, police say robbery was the motive. But privately, they have already begun investigating Roger and Marjorie Caldwell, Miss Congdon's daughter and son-in-law.

July 6, 1977:
Police arrest Roger Caldwell and charge him with committing the murders, allegedly to speed the collection of his wife's hefty share of the inheritance.

July 15, 1977:
University of Minnesota officials, who now own the Congdon Mansion under the terms of Miss Congdon's will, discuss what to do with the property. Some suggestions: a Scandinavian resource center, a retreat for the arts or a center for the study of Lake Superior. Eventually, officials decide to offer tours of the mansion, which prove to be very successful.

Sept. 6, 1977:
Four of Marjorie Caldwell's seven children from a previous marriage ask a court to disqualify their mother from sharing in the inheritance, if she is involved in the murders.

April 10, 1978:
Roger Caldwell's murder trial begins in Brainerd, Mn., moved from Duluth because of extensive publicity. It takes nearly a month to pick a jury and then there are two months of testimony.

July 8, 1978:
After three days of deliberations, the jury finds Caldwell guilty of both murders.

July 10, 1978:
Caldwell is sentenced to two consecutive life terms in prison.

July 11, 1978:
Encouraged by Roger's conviction, officials in Duluth charge Marjorie Caldwell with conspiring to kill her mother and the nurse. She is released on $100,000 bond.

April 2, 1979:
Marjorie Caldwell's trial begins in Hastings, Mn., again moved because of pre-trial publicity.

July 21, 1979:
The jury deliberates nine hours and finds Marjorie not guilty of the charges. After the trial, the jurors throw a party and invite Marjorie.

July 25, 1979:
Roger Caldwell's attorney asks for a new trial, based on new evidence from his wife's trial.

Aug. 7, 1981:
Marjorie Caldwell weds Wallace Hagen of Mound, Mn., in Valley City, N.D., Roger Caldwell doesn't learn of the wedding for two years, and claims he and Marjorie were never divorced.

Aug. 6, 1982:
The Minnesota Supreme Court grants Roger Caldwell a new trial, citing the new evidence from Marjorie's trial. Roger is released from prison after serving more than five years, and goes home to Latrobe, Pa., to await a new trial.

March 20, 1983:
North Dakota officials charge Marjorie Caldwell with bigamy. She will not be extradited, they say, so she faces arrest only if she returns to North Dakota.

May 31, 1983:
Marjorie Caldwell and her children reach an out-of-court settlement in the inheritance dispute. She gets one-fourth of a family trust set up by her mother and she will draw the income from one-third of her children's share until she dies. A good chunk of the inheritance, though, perhaps as much as $2 million, goes for attorney's fees.

July 5, 1983:
Roger Caldwell and Duluth officials agree to a plea bargain in the murder case: Roger pleads guilty to second degree murder. In return, he does not have to serve any more time in prison.

Jan. 13, 1984:
Marjorie Caldwell Hagen is convicted of arson and insurance fraud in connection with a 1982 fire at a house in Mound, Mn. She is sentenced to 2½ years in prison.

Jan. 26, 1985:
Her appeal is turned down, so Marjorie begins serving her time for the arson and fraud conviction. She is released 21 months later.

May 17, 1988:
Roger Caldwell kills himself in a small Latrobe apartment, where he lived with a girlfriend. Only nine people attend his funeral three days later.

Mar. 24, 1991:
Marjorie is arrested in Ajo, Az., and charged with trying to burn down her neighbor's house. Police suspect her in 13 other suspicious fires in the small retirement community near the Mexican border, where she lives with ailing husband Wally.

Oct. 29, 1992:
Marjorie is convicted of attempted arson. Although she is supposed to go immediately to jail, she convinces the judge to give her 24 hours of freedom "to take care of Wally."

Oct. 30, 1992:
Wally Hagen is found dead in his home. At first, police believe he's been gassed to death and Marjorie is arrested and charged with murder. Later, police say he died of a drug overdose, a possible suicide. The murder charges were dropped due to a lack of evidence, but Marjorie is sentenced to 15 years in prison on the attempted arson conviction.

Nov. 15, 2001:
After serving nine years on the attempted arson term, Marjorie attends her first parole hearing. Two of Wally's children – who believe Marjorie killed their dad – attend the proceedings to urge her continued confinement. One of Marjorie's children and Marjorie's sister also request in writing that parole be denied. The parole board agrees and refuses to grant her early release.

Jan. 5, 2004:
After nearly 11 years in prison, Marjorie was released from the Arizona State Prison at Perryville. A rented limo picked her up and zoomed off to the east, toward Tucson. The driver is able to speed away from media cars trying to follow. Marjorie's sister warns: "I'm worried she'll do something awful again."

Mar. 4, 2009:
Marjorie is sentenced to probation after pleading guilty in a fraud case. Police said she bilked an elderly man's estate after he died.

The
Author

Joe Kimball, an award-winning reporter for the Minneapolis Star Tribune, happened to be in Duluth on the day of the Congdon murders and is still writing about the story nearly three decades later.

Kimball is the only reporter to cover the case from beginning to end, the only reporter to testify at the murder trial, the only reporter to attend Marjorie Hagen's parole hearing and the only non-family member present at Roger Caldwell's funeral after his suicide.

Kimball's candid insights on these and other exclusive moments have made Secrets of the Congdon Mansion a regional best seller and Kimball the recognized expert on the case.

This publication was produced, illustrated, and designed by Albarella Design, Inc., South St. Paul, MN